MEDIUM ÆVUM MONOGRAPHS
NEW SERIES XI

NINE VERSE SERMONS
BY NICHOLAS BOZON

The Art of an Anglo-Norman Poet and Preacher

BRIAN J. LEVY

Lecturer in French
at the University of Hull

The Society for the Study of
Mediæval Languages and Literature
Oxford
1981

British Library Cataloguing in Publication Data

Bozon, Nicholas
    Nine verse sermons. — (Medium Aevum monographs. New
    series; 11)
    1. Bozon, Nicholas — Sermons
    2. Sermons, French
    I. Title   II. Levy, Brian J.   III. Series
    252'.00944   BV4254.F/
    ISBN 0-907570-01-1

Typeset by Anne Joshua Associates

PREFACE

I should like to record my thanks to Professor C. E. Pickford and to Professor R. C. Johnston who both took on the task of reading my work in typescript, and whose suggestions and words of encouragement I found equally valuable. My thanks are also due to Mr P. C. McClure of the Department of English, University of Hull, for his help and advice on various Middle English matters, and to the participants in the 1980 Oxford Symposium of the Society for Medieval Sermon Studies, whose pertinent comments and questions provided me with very useful last-minute notes.

I gratefully acknowledge the ready assistance received from the British Library (Manuscript Division) and from the Lambeth Palace Library.

B.J.L.

CONTENTS

PREFACE iii

ABBREVIATIONS vi

INTRODUCTION 1

MANUSCRIPT AND TEXT 17

NICHOLAS BOZON'S NINE VERSE SERMONS 21

THE FIRST SERMON: On Preachers and Sunrays 25

THE SECOND SERMON: The Twin Banquets 35

THE THIRD SERMON: Dancing Down to Hell 45

THE FOURTH SERMON: Man's Contrary Nature 51

THE FIFTH SERMON: Harvest of Life 59

THE SIXTH SERMON: On Foolish Chatter 65

THE SEVENTH SERMON: The Useless Will 71

THE EIGHTH SERMON: Prepare for Death 77

THE NINTH SERMON: The Humble and the Hypocritical 87

CONCLUSION 99

ABBREVIATIONS

ASNS	*Archiv für das Studium der neueren Sprachen*
CFMA	Les Classiques français du moyen âge
DNB	*Dictionary of National Biography*
EETS	Early English Text Society
HLF	*Histoire littéraire de la France*
JEGP	*Journal of English and Germanic Philology*
MLN	*Modern Language Notes*
SATF	Société des anciens textes français
SPh	*Studies in Philology*
TLF	Textes littéraires français

INTRODUCTION

The aim of this monograph is the presentation and critical analysis of a series of nine short Anglo-Norman verse sermons composed by Friar Nicholas Bozon, a prolific author who flourished at the end of the thirteenth century and in the early part of the fourteenth. The poems are all found together in a single manuscript (MS British Library Additional 46919); however one, the eighth in the sequence, is also extant in an important variant version preserved in two other manuscripts (MSS Lambeth Palace Library 522 and British Library Sloane 1611). They remain as a whole unedited: P. Meyer lists them, with extracts, in his 'notice' of the manuscript,[1] and three of the pieces are included in a soon-to-be published survey of Anglo-Norman poetry.[2]

Very little is known of Nicholas Bozon, save what may be practically gleaned from the internal evidence of his compositions, or from the frequent introductory rubrics to individual texts.[3] He was a Franciscan, *del ordre de freres menours*, and he states specifically that he was *ordenours*: that is, a friar enjoying the right to administer absolution (a right coveted by the mendicants, and the cause of considerable friction between them and other members of the clergy who saw their powers usurped). His home ground was the English North Midlands of the counties of Nottingham, Leicester and Derby; he was most probably a member of the large and influential Franciscan Friary at Nottingham, which had been founded by 1230, within six years of the arrival of the first Friars in England. As the Nottingham house was under the Oxford custody, he very likely went on

[1] 'Notice et extraits du Ms. 8336 de la Bibliothèque de Sir Thomas Phillips, à Cheltenham', *Romania*, 13 (1884), 497–541.

[2] D. L. Jeffrey and B. J. Levy, *The Anglo-Norman Lyric* (Ottawa University Press).

[3] M. Hewlett, 'A medieval Popular Preacher', *The Nineteenth Century*, 28 (1890), 472–73. Sister M. A. Klenke: 'Nicholas Bozon', *Speculum*, 15 (1940), 444–53; *Nicholas Bozon: Three Saints' Lives* (New. York, 1947); *Seven More Poems by Nicholas Bozon* (New York, 1951); 'An Anglo-Norman Gospel Poem by Nicholas Bozon', *SPh*, 48 (1951), 250–66; 'Nicholas Bozon', *MLN*, 69 (1954), 256–60; 'Steventon Priory and a Bozon Manuscript', *Speculum*, 30 (1955), 218–21; 'Nicholas Bozon', in *Dictionnaire des Lettres françaises: Le moyen âge* (Paris, 1964), p. 549. M. D. Legge: *Anglo-Norman in the Cloisters* (Edinburgh U.P., 1950), pp. 85–89; *Anglo-Norman Literature and its Background* (Oxford, 1963), pp. 229–32. P. Meyer and L. Toulmin Smith, *Les Contes moralisés de Nicole Bozon* (Paris, SATF, 1889). A. Thomas, 'Nicole Bozon', in *HLF*, XXXVI (1924), 400–24. This bibliography does not include all editions of works by Bozon but is limited to items containing specific biographical details.

to Oxford to study: his works certainly show him well-versed in a wide range of matters, and quite possibly influenced by the teachings of Robert Grosseteste who in the years 1229–30 had been appointed first lecturer to the Franciscans at Oxford. He also reveals some knowledge of the North Country (mentioning in one of his works the old Yorkshire term 'wapentake' to denote a local division of land): reasonably enough, as Nottingham was in the York diocese.

The form of his name varies in his works and their attributory rubrics: *Bozon, Bosoun, Bojoun/Boioun, Boun.* A good case may be made for his belonging to the Bozons of Norfolk, a distinguished county family boasting the old heraldic insignia of the 'Boujon' or crossbow bolt, and from whose ranks, at the beginning of the fourteenth century, came a number of priests.

Bozon has left us far more to consider on the bibliographical side than on the biographical: Professor Legge has called him 'probably the most prolific of Anglo-Norman writers',[4] and the claim is hardly unjustified. A quick glance at his extant works – all in French, but clearly indicating the knowledge both of Latin and of common English that is such a linguistic feature of the educated England of Edward I – reveals a composer of considerable ability, interests and stamina. In prose he wrote a highly entertaining collection of *Contes moralisés*: 145 little tales, some plain exempla, others two-part stories with a moral narrative followed by a supporting cautionary anecdote. These stories, drawing for inspiration from the great common stock of popular lore, Scripture, glosses, Bestiaries, fables and fabliaux, would have provided suitable material for the sermons in which the mendicants took such great pride and to which they attached such great importance. Here Bozon follows in the general tradition of such scholars as Petrus Lombardus, Petrus Comestor, Etienne de Bourbon, Alain de Lille and Jacques de Vitry, whose compilations and preaching manuals (such as the *Summa de arte praedicatoria*, the *Sermones vulgares* and the *Sermones communes*) were the stuff of moralising sermons and improving exempla from the early thirteenth century onwards. More specifically, the *Contes* round off an important series of Franciscan (and mainly Anglo-Norman) collections of exempla (*Liber exemplorum, Tabula exemplorum, Speculum laicorum*), of which further mention will be made, and which also provide parallel illustrations of certain key themes in Bozon's verse sermons.

Nicholas Bozon's verse output may be classified under a number of headings. He composed a complex Gospel Poem on the love of God, and a handful of poems of Marial devotion: two *Aves*, a prayer of supplication,

---

[4] *Anglo-Norman in the Cloisters*, p. 86.

an *Annunciation* and a *Plainte Nostre-Dame*. He composed no fewer than eleven Saints' lives, drawing extensively from the *Legenda aurea* of Jacobus de Voragine. Other works are allegorical: Bozon follows a well-trodden path with a *Debat de l'Yver et de l'Esté* (although the attribution here is by no means certain) and a *Desputeyson du cors et de l'alme*; he is also the author of a very interesting *Allegory of the Passion* that exists in both a long and a short version, and of two poems on Pride (*Le Char d'Orgueil* and *La Lettre de l'Empereur Orgueil*).

The telling satire and criticism of the vices of the 'siècle' found in these last two poems are taken up again to excellent effect in the final category of Bozon's works: a series of poems unmasking certain social and moral failings, proposing a true conduct of life and making a cautionary point that is somewhat sharper than are those found in the massed exempla of the *Contes moralisés*. Chief among these texts is the long *Plainte d'Amour*, Bozon's poetic masterpiece: it is a fine full-blooded social satire on the corruption of Church and State, evidently inspired by Clement V's Bull of 1312, *Exivi de paradiso*, in which the Pope urged upon the Franciscans ever more examples of asceticism and self-denial. The poet mines a less rare didactic vein in his *Proverbes de bon enseignement*, a series of quatrains glossing a number of improving Latin tags; and he expresses a common medieval dualism in two opposing poems on women: one, *Les femmes a la pie* . . . being a raucous antifeminist satire with much of the fabliau about it, while the other, *De la bounté des femmes*, is an exercise in redressing the balance, showing the virtues of women in their proper place, obeying the 'natural' rules imposed upon them. Human failings and obligations also form the essential subject-matter of an effective little *tretis* on 'Denaturesse' (evil, unnatural behaviour), and of the sequence of verse sermons that are here discussed: each of the nine independent poems neatly captures and exemplifies a homiletical point, sometimes in allegory, but always in plain language.

That Bozon must have been a well-known and popular author-preacher in the England of his day is attested partly by the manuscript rubrics that so frequently claim such and such a work as his, and also by the number of Anglo-Norman manuscripts in which his *oeuvre* is preserved (although MS British Library Additional 46919 remains the single most precious repository of his work): three copies of the *Contes moralisés*, four of the *Char d'Orgueil* and the *Desputeyson*, seven of the *Plainte d'Amour*, and nine of the *Proverbes de bon enseignement*.

Nicholas Bozon's popularity is deserved: in all his works he shows himself a versatile and intelligent composer, an observer of the human condition as well as Franciscan moraliser upon it. His originality is not in his

basic material which has inevitably been culled from many expected
sources and follows some of the conventional routes of medieval didactic
literature; it lies rather in his approach and treatment. In dealing with
human failings he comes down to earth, and quotes very practical, everyday examples; and he shows a rather touching understanding and compassion that add a humanising dimension to his allegories, his cautionary tales
and his satirical attacks. Through him we have a particularly fine view of a
gifted medieval friar at work, preaching and illustrating his ideals in verse
and prose. He can turn his hand to many themes, and has the not incon-
siderable wit to tailor his chosen verse-form to a given subject; he has a
penchant for the Anglo-Norman tail-rhyme, but is equally at home with
the quatrain, the monorhyme, the couplet, long lines and short. In his
otherwise fine survey of Bozon's works, A. Thomas shows a most unjust
continental contempt for the Anglo-Norman composer: 'prenons garde de
nous laisser piper en lui attribuant plus de mérite qu'il n'en a . . . presque
rien, pourtant, dans tous ces vers, ne s'élève au-dessus de la médiocrité . . .'.[5]
Nicholas Bozon deserves more serious and more appreciative consideration: being large, his output has its patchiness; but at their best his prose
and verse works are excellent. Indeed, in his versatility he merits mention
in the same breath as the great Rutebeuf: he too composes antifeminist
jibes and ardent prayers to the Virgin, Saints' lives (including, coinci-
dentally, a Life of Elizabeth of Hungary, also one of Rutebeuf's subjects),
allegories on the state of the 'siècle', and cutting social satires, all in a
variety of poetic patterns. This poetic flexibility is very observable even in
the limited compass of his little verse sermons, and says much for his
inventive mind. It is not a little ironic that this most prolific fourteenth-
century Anglo-Norman Franciscan should be in many respects the literary
brother of the great thirteenth-century French opponent of the 'frères
cordeliers' and all the other Orders of mendicants.

* * *

In order to set Bozon and his verse sermons in their historical context
a brief account of the presence and activity of the early Grey Friars in
England is necessary.[6] The Franciscan mission in England had begun on

---

[5] 'Nicole Bozon', pp. 409, 412.
[6] A. G. Little, *Studies in English Franciscan History* (Manchester U.P., 1917);
J. R. H. Moorman, *History of the Franciscan Order* (Oxford, 1968), *The Franciscans
in England* (London and Oxford, 1974); D. L. Jeffrey, *The Early English Lyric and
Franciscan Spirituality* (University of Nebraska Press, 1975).

10 September 1224, when nine Friars disembarked at Dover, led by Agnellus of Pisa who had been custodian of the Paris house; in his small party were three Englishmen: Richard of Ingworth, Richard of Devon and William of Esseby. They made straight for Canterbury where, being hospitably received by the monks of Christ Church, they set up their first rudimentary house; while Agnellus stayed to foster the infant community with four of his companions, the other Franciscans journeyed on to London, there to establish a second house with the help of the Dominicans who had settled in England before them. Both communities flourished with the speed that had marked the rise of the order in Italy and in France; their four key ideals — poverty, humility, simplicity and prayer — which had found keen responses throughout Europe, were particularly suited to appeal to an England still feeling the shock of the Great Interdict, and eager for spiritual reform.

The Franciscans were above all mobile: in 1225 they moved on from London to Oxford, to attract the equally peripatetic student community; by 1233 there were some forty friars at the University, many attending the new school in which Robert Grosseteste was teaching. A similar theological school was soon after set up at Cambridge; in England as on the continent the Order was attracting men of scholarship, and the articulate intelligence of such English Grey Friars as Nicholas Bozon may be seen as widespread, and part of a continuous development. Indeed, four of the greatest figures of medieval Franciscan learning were British: Alexander of Hales, Roger Bacon, Duns Scotus and William of Ockham.

Between 1225 and 1230 Franciscan houses were established in a dozen cathedral cities, ports and towns, as far north as York and as far west as Bristol; to this period belongs the foundation of the Nottingham house:[7] the Order had already assured itself of the goodwill of the king, and Henry III himself made a grant of a score of tie-beams for the construction of the Franciscan chapel at Nottingham, in 1230. Ten years later, William of Nottingham, who had spent some time in Rome, was appointed 'Provincial minister', or leader of the whole Franciscan community of England.

By the middle of the thirteenth century there were over 1200 Franciscans in England, spread over forty-nine friaries; most of them were ordained, and in their growing numbers and evangelism had introduced a new and very telling element into the spiritual life of the country. As they moved among the people, preaching, teaching and hearing confessions, there was conflict with the local clergy who naturally came to look upon them more as poachers than brothers; the members of the older established orders also

[7] Cf. D. M. Knowles and R. N. Hadcock, *Medieval Religious Houses in England* (London, 1953; new edition 1971), p. 227.

gazed suspiciously at the newcomers, with their fresh spirituality and their insistence on a renewal of purity and poverty that seemed to mock their own power and wealth. Just as the increasing influence of the mendicant orders in French church and academic politics had, by the middle of the thirteenth century, brought hostile reaction from such critics as Guillaume de Saint-Amour and the masters of the University of Paris, and their most articulate supporter Rutebeuf, so in England, as the thirteenth century gave way to the fourteenth, the Franciscan Order found itself by its very success under attack on the grounds of hypocrisy, of failing to live up to its own rule of poverty. Thus there arose the stereotyped portrait of the friar too willing to grant absolution in order to receive a sinner's generous donation; and Chaucer's famous condemnation of the corrupt Friar, 'an esy man to yeve penaunce / Ther as he wiste to have a good pitaunce',[8] echoes with uncomfortable precision the earlier savage hostility of Rutebeuf and the French antimendicant poets of the previous century.[9] Nevertheless, the influence of the Franciscans remained very great, for the public as a whole still welcomed their mission and their presence; and this was in no small way due to the skill with which the friars deployed their great weapon of direct communication, the sermon.

* * *

From the start of their mission in England, the Franciscans headed for the largest centres of population; they sought out the poor people, and the townsfolk, to whom they might preach their essential Gospel message. St Francis himself had stressed the vital importance of the sermon in the practical work of the Order, and according to Bernardino of Siena, the sermon was more essential even than the mass.[10] The German friar Berthold von Regensburg declared roundly that his job was to preach: *Predigen ist min amt . . . ;*[11] and in a famous letter sent to Pope Gregory IX in 1238, Robert Grosseteste praises the Franciscans in England for the

    [8] *Canterbury Tales*, edited by F. N. Robinson (*Complete Works of Chaucer*, Oxford, 2nd edition, 1957), *Prologue*, vv. 223–24.
    [9] Compare Rutebeuf, *La Bataille des Vices contre les Vertus*, vv. 94–96: 'Se sainte Yglise escommenie / Li Frere pueent bien assaudre / S'escommeniez a que saudre . . .' (edited by E. Faral and J. Bastin, Paris, 1969).
    [10] Little, p. 133.
    [11] H. Thode, *Franz von Assisi und die Anfänge der Kunst der Renaissance in Italien* (Berlin, 1904), p. 415.

zeal and effect of their preaching and teaching.[12] Grosseteste's own role of Oxford teacher to the Franciscans themselves shows again the fair premium set in the Order upon learning, for very practical reasons: the best sermon is given by the most articulate preacher, and the friars soon became famed for their knowledge, as *sacrae paginae doctores, scil. predicatores, qui habent nos instruere.*[13] As much as anything else, it was the ability of the friars to preach a powerful sermon (while cutting the length of other portions of the church service) that gathered the crowds into faithful congregations up and down the country. Church building inevitably reflects ritual; and friary churches tended to be large and spacious affairs, with open naves enabling the largest possible number of people to attend and to focus their attention upon the pulpit. More than one medieval commentator remarks upon the 'large and wide chirchis whiche religiose persoones, namelich of the begging religiouns, maken, that therebi the more multitude of persoones mowe be recevyed togidere, for to here theryn prechingis to be made in reyne daies . . .'.[14] Despite the rather jaundiced views of their opponents, and despite their own criticisms — often trenchant, as we shall see — of inattention and lack of decorum, the Franciscans employed their sermons to great effect. A number of little anecdotes, current from the thirteenth century, bear popular witness to the power of the itinerant preacher: how a friar cured a paralytic whose groans had been heard throughout his sermon; or how a wanton's heart broke under the effect of the preacher's words, and how, on being restored to life, the words 'Ave Maria' were found printed on her tongue as she made her sincere confession.[15]

The need for true confession was always an essential theme of Franciscan sermons; the Order's insistence on the spirituality of 'holy poverty' contained within it the moralising injunction to turn away from wealth and other worldly considerations, and to adopt all the modest and simple virtues. The sinner could cleanse himself through contrition, confession and penitence; and the preacher's message would often enough be a call to repent, addressed to all classes of society. This theme of repentance runs through medieval thought, on many levels,[16] and is at its most intense

---

[12] *Epistolae*, edited by H. Luard (London, Rolls Series, 1861), pp. 179–80. As will be seen, this detail is of particular significance when one reads Bozon's first verse sermon.

[13] *Gesta Romanorum*, quoted in G. R. Owst, *Preaching in Medieval England* (Cambridge, 1926), p. 3.

[14] Bishop Pecock, *Repressor*, edited by C. Babington (London, Rolls Series, 1860), II, 553.

[15] Owst, *Preaching in Medieval England*, p. 57.

[16] See J. C. Payen, *Le Motif du repentir dans la littérature française médiévale* (Geneva, 1967).

in the thirteenth century; and much of the evangelical work of the Franciscans and the other Orders follows on from the legislation of the Fourth
Lateran Council of 1215. This council was the product of the reforming
zeal of Innocent III who wished to combat the three greatest threats to
Christendom: from the march of Islam in the Holy Land (Jerusalem having
fallen after the defeat at Hattin in 1187), from the growth of heresy (in
particular Albigensianism), and from increasing social and clerical deca-
dence and over-worldliness. His introductory Bull 'Vineam Domini' of
1213 clearly stated his aims of crushing heretical falsehoods and extirpat-
ing vices, and replacing them with orthodox truth and virtue.[17] Accordingly, the Council drew up a new constitution of the faith, *De fide catholica*,
insisting upon the uniqueness of the true church in offering salvation, and
stressing the importance of the sacraments and of penitence, in an atmosphere of properly-ordained orthodoxy. Lateran IV then promulgated a
number of decrees, among the most significant being a programme of
preaching laid upon each diocese, and the injunction that the faithful
should go to confession at least once a year, should carry out the required
penance and receive the sacrament (particularly at Eastertide).

The way was now clear for the new movements to flourish, all the more
so because the friars enjoyed the ear and the goodwill of the Pope, and
were more manifestly helping to advance the cause of the Council. In
England, the Lateran legislation – doubly impressive following the crushing effect of the Interdict – was reinforced by the Statutes of Salisbury, as
finally promulgated at the Council of Oxford in 1222: emphasis was laid
on the teaching of the faith to congregations, by means of instructive
sermons in the vernacular.

In England, as in France and Germany, a pattern was clearly established:
the friars invariably used the vernacular when preaching to their large lay
congregations. Latin was employed for sermons addressed to scholars,
monks and fellow-clerics in general; and sometimes a sermon originally
preached in English might later be set down in Latin for the purpose of
instruction: it would thus become incorporated into the growing body
of Latin material aimed at improving a preacher's sermon-technique.

* * *

From the twelfth century it had been recognised that a good sermon,
to be effective, had to be illustrated; and it was here that the medieval

[17] For details of the Council, see R. Foreville, *Latran I, II, III et Latran IV*
(Histoire des conciles oecuméniques, 6: Paris, 1965), pp. 227–386.

exemplum came into its own.[18] With subjects chosen at will from Scripture, commentaries, Saints' lives, fables and from contemporary anecdotes, the exempla provided the sermon with a very necessary dramatic dimension. They might be purely approbatory, recounting the improving details of the life and acts of such and such a Father of the Church; or they might be cautionary, telling of the damning effect of vice, of the fall of a sinner, checked perhaps by contrition and penance. One of the scholars most influential in spreading the popularity of the exemplum was Jacques de Vitry, bishop of Acre and Cardinal of Tusculum, who spent most of his life after his ordination in 1210 involved in crusading missions, against the Saracens in the Holy Land and against the Albigensian heresy. He was the most celebrated preacher of his day, and his work survives in the *Sermones feriales et communes* and the *Sermones vulgares*; these sermons, addressing a wide range of social classes, from fellow-clergy to artisans and farmers, are studded with suitable exempla. Found in 'shorthand form' in manuscripts of the sermons, these exempla were very popular, and were expanded and circulated independently in other manuscripts of the thirteenth and fourteenth centuries.[19] Among the first preachers to be directly influenced by Jacques de Vitry was a Dominican friar, Etienne de Bourbon (d. 1261), who had also been involved in the Albigensian Crusade, and who composed the earliest compendium of massed exempla as a preaching aid, the *Tractatus de diversis materiis predicabilibus*[20] (in which he stresses the importance of the genre, and frequently cites Jacques de Vitry as source).

With Etienne the friars had become involved in the scholarly production of exempla-collections; and by the second half of the century Franciscan hands had begun an influential series of compendia consisting of various exempla neatly classified and listed alphabetically under subject-matter. These works are mainly English in origin, and reveal the strength of learning that was a keystone to the Anglo-Norman province; they form a coherent chain of Franciscan teaching leading up to Nicholas Bozon, and beyond.

The earliest is the *Liber exemplorum*,[21] composed between 1275 and 1279 by a Warwickshire friar working frequently in Ireland. It comprises

---

[18] The standard work on the subject is J. Th. Welter, *L'Exemplum dans la littérature religieuse et didactique du moyen âge* (Paris and Toulouse, 1927).

[19] *The Exempla . . . from the Sermones Vulgares of Jacques de Vitry*, edited by T. F. Crane (New York, 1890; reprint, 1971); J. Greven, *Die Exempla aus den Sermones feriales et communes des Jakob von Vitry* (Heidelberg, 1914).

[20] See Welter, *L'Exemplum . . .* , pp. 215–23.

[21] *Liber exemplorum ad usum praedicantium*, edited by A. G. Little (Aberdeen, 1908).

213 exempla, spread over two main sections: one on Christian dogma, the other on moral teaching; this second part contains thirty-eight rubrics in alphabetical order (the text breaks off at 'M', as the one extant manuscript is incomplete). Although there is, rather surprisingly, nothing specifically Franciscan in the contents, the various exempla present a standard array of virtues and vices, with a leavening of personally-gathered anecdotes giving quite a vivid insight into itinerant life in Ireland.

A second collection, compiled around the same time (in the late 1270s), is the *Tabula exemplorum*,[22] containing over 300 exempla. It is of French origin, and its popularity is attested by its survival in over twenty manuscripts spanning three centuries; its author, a fairly down-to-earth 'Cordelier de province', provides under each subject-heading a little commentary-cum-definition, leaning heavily upon the work of Etienne de Bourbon but also making some sharp observations on the contemporary way of the world; this is then followed by suitable exempla, as often as not in skeletal form. The overall impression is one of realism and practical observation; the Latin text is punctuated here and there by French proverbs and expressions, and the entries pointing a cautionary finger at the vices of society have something in common with the powerful moralising and satirical OF poems of the thirteenth century (such as Guiot de Provins's *Bible*, or the *Besant Dieu* of Guillaume le Clerc). The *Tabula* is patently the work of a friar mingling with society and tailoring his comments accordingly.

The influence of the *Tabula exemplorum* is to be seen in the third alphabetical compilation, the *Speculum laicorum*,[23] composed between the years 1279 and 1292. The author is an Englishman, probably from Kent; and his preaching itineraries up the East coast may be clearly traced from the wealth of topographical detail he provides by way of local colour: his text contains references to Canterbury, London, Norwich, Cambridge, Ely, Lincoln, York and Berwick-upon-Tweed; and he also appears to have struck west, into Hampshire and Oxfordshire. He is extremely methodical, and his work is a model of documentation and presentation. His intention has been to provide a complete and convenient portable handbook for the busy friar, to help him in his sermons (he states as much in a brisk prologue). He draws up an alphabetical table for ease of reference; each entry is introduced by pithy definitions, neatly subdivided into categories, and followed by various one-line citings of scriptural or ecclesiastical authorities; then come the exempla. This expert format, a fine blend of the erudite and the entertaining (the author makes passing allusion to young people's love of football and to the notorious drunkenness of the common

---

[22] *Tabula exemplorum secundum ordinem alphabeti*, edited by J. Th. Welter (Paris, 1927).   [23] Edited by J. Th. Welter (Paris, 1914).

Englishman, and often praises the Franciscan mission while showing the established clergy in a somewhat poor light), was clearly popular: the *Speculum laicorum* exists in nineteen copies, and gives us a very fair impression of the state of Franciscan preaching in England during the first half of the reign of Edward I.

The late thirteenth century saw a further collection of exempla put together by an English Franciscan; untitled, it survives in a single copy on fols 1–213 of MS 35 in the Bibliothèque municipale, Auxerre,[24] and may be dated to 1279–92. It contains no fewer than 414 exempla, and must have proved a rather deep mine of information.

With the early fourteenth century, this brief survey of Franciscan exempla-collections reaches Nicholas Bozon, whose *Contes moralisés* may be seen to be very much in the tradition. He has not adopted the alphabetical system, but his improving anecdotes all fall under rubrics itemising particular virtues and vices; and his aim, in common with his predecessors, is to produce a manual for sermon-making: 'En ceo petit liveret poet l'em trover meynt beal ensaumple de diverse matiere par ont l'em poet aprendre de eschuer peché, de embracer bontee, e sur tote rien de loer Dampnedee. . . .'[25] Indeed a number of his longer stories bear all the marks of having been employed by Bozon himself in his own sermons, and subsequently tailored into the collection. The nine verse sermons bear added witness to Bozon's skill as a practitioner as well as compiler and teacher; and it will be seen how frequently the poet's choice of subject-matter or use of imagery finds parallel echoes among the exempla, not merely of his own *Contes*, but also of the earlier Franciscan collections.

The fourteenth century produced three more large-scale works of English scholarship in the field of the mendicant exemplum. A near-contemporary of Bozon's *Contes* is the *Fasciculus morum*,[26] probably composed c. 1320 by a Franciscan, John Spiser, and revised by another Greyfriar, Robert Silke (or Selke: the rather ambiguous attributions are made in four of the twenty-one extant MSS); from local references in the text, it would appear that the author knew the area around Coventry and Shrewsbury, in the custody of the Worcester friary of which he was presumably a member. The collection contains many of the vivid images of everyday life that are such a feature of the 'English school'.

Dating from c. 1340, the *Gesta Romanorum*[27] was to prove the most internationally celebrated of all the collections; it is technically the work

---

[24] The text is unedited; see Welter, *L'Exemplum* . . . , pp. 301–04, and Moorman, *History of the Franciscan Order*, p. 272.

[25] See the edition by Meyer and Toulmin Smith, p. 8.

[26] Unedited; see Little, *Studies* . . . , pp. 139–57.

[27] Edited by H. Oesterley (Berlin, 1872); cf. Welter, *L'Exemplum* . . . , pp. 369–75.

of a German friar, but all its material clearly indicates an English Franciscan origin: indeed, among its direct sources are the *Speculum laicorum*
and Bozon's *Contes moralisés*. Its net is a very wide one: ancient history
and legend are added to the animal stories and the improving and cautionary anecdotes. The Latin text survives in at least 138 manuscripts, and was
translated into a number of vernaculars, including — appropriately enough
— English.

The final collection is the most massive of all, containing well over
a thousand exempla spread through 189 alphabetically-arranged headings.
It is the *Summa predicantium*,[28] dating from the second half of the fourteenth century and composed by a Dominican friar, John de Bromyard of
Herefordshire, who was chancellor of the University of Cambridge in the
1380s. With Bromyard the criticism of aspects of society contained in all
the friars' moralising collections moves on to the sharper level of satire and
complaint, and paves the way for the more frankly political writings of the
fifteenth century. John Bromyard is vituperative in his various indictments
of social injustices; he wields his exempla like so many weapons, and he is
also a mine of information concerning customs and practices, not only in
England but also culled from his journeys in France and Italy.

By the fifteenth century the friars were producing writings in English,
departing from the Latin of the previous collections. It is worth noting
that the earliest extant example of this move towards the vernacular is
in fact Nicholas Bozon's *Contes moralisés*; indeed, Bozon is doubly unusual
in being the only composer of a preaching-aid in Anglo-Norman: he seems
to be aiming at an audience of intelligent, educated lay classes as well as
fellow-friars. Certainly, as will be seen, these people form the 'congregation' of his Verse Sermons; and as Bozon is a continual user of Anglo-
Norman in his works, the implication is that his mission found him in
regular contact with French-speaking society. It is interesting to note
that two fellow friars and poets chose to compose in English. The first,
Bozon's contemporary, was William Herebert, of the Hereford house, who
became lector at Oxford, and died in 1333.[29] He was celebrated for his
powerful sermons, some of which, in Latin, have been preserved; but
he also translated into English numerous hymns and carols, possibly to
include in sermons by way of vernacular liturgical accompaniment before
a popular audience. It will be shown that he knew Bozon's work, and had

[28] A number of MSS of the text exist, and its continued popularity is shown by
some early editions: notably Bâle, 1479, Nuremberg, 1485 and 1518, Paris, 1518 and
Lyons, 1522. A study of Bromyard's work is to be found in G. R. Owst, *Literature
and Pulpit in Medieval England* (Oxford, 1961); see also Welter, *L'Exemplum . . . ,*
pp. 328–34.

[29] See *DNB*, IX, 669: 'Herbert'.

in particular read the Verse Sermons, of which he translated one text into English verse.

The other, rather later, Franciscan 'populariser' was friar John Grimestone, who compiled in 1372 a preacher's Commonplace Book[30] for pulpit use; it is not unlike the great exempla-collections, being mainly in Latin, and alphabetical, but it contains many English rhymes and poems, heavily influenced by Franciscan spirituality.

This, then, is the homiletic background to Nicholas Bozon's nine Verse Sermons. It is appropriate at this point, before studying the poems themselves and the manuscript in which they appear, to consider briefly the phenomenon of the sermon in verse, the 'Reimpredigt'. The use of rhyme, either in the form of snatches of verse studding a prose sermon, or in a whole poem preaching a given theme, would be calculated to add drama to the pulpit; the verse form stresses eloquence over any detailed, subtle elaboration: it lends itself to the forceful expression of essentials, and is a fine device to attract and hold the attention of a lay audience. Verse is for the populariser, and its increasing use, first in Latin and subsequently in the vernacular, was looked at with huge disfavour by some thirteenth-century purists who attacked it as a frivolous, new-fangled debasement of the true art of pulpit rhetoric. According to Pierre de Limoges, verse sermons appeal more to the ear than to the soul, with their puerile language and jingling rhythms; they turn a preacher into an actor: *quae praedicatio theatralis est et inimica animae*.[31] Despite such criticisms other preachers, like the friars, who were intent on appealing to the people in simple, yet powerful terms, saw the potential of verse, and encouraged its presence in sermons.[32]

The OF verse sermon, as a recognisable genre, dates from the late twelfth century.[33] The earliest texts – *Grant Mal fist Adan*, Guichard de Beaulieu's *Sermon*, Hélinant de Froidmont's *Vers de la Mort* (which, we shall see, Bozon knows and uses for inspiration) – are strongly minatory in content, dwelling with often macabre details on the horrors of Hell, and showing the appalling grim features of Death who comes to all. From the beginning of the thirteenth century, the aim of the verse sermon shifts crucially, from merely inspiring dread of Hell to inculcating the need for repentance

[30] Edinburgh, Advocates' Library MS 18. 7. 21; examples of the songs may be found in F. Carleton-Brown, *English Religious Lyrics of the Fourteenth Century* (Oxford, 1924), and in E. Wilson, *A Descriptive Index of the English Lyrics in John of Grimestone's Preaching Book*, Medium Aevum Monographs NS.2 (Oxford, 1973).

[31] A. Lecoy de la Marche, *La Chaire française au moyen âge* (Paris, 1886), pp. 279–80 and *passim*.

[32] Owst, *Preaching in Medieval England*, pp 273–78.

[33] J. C. Payen provides a good survey of this 'prédication par la crainte' in *Le Motif du repentir . . .*, pp. 489–515.

in order to escape the fires. The use of allegory and exempla abounds to this effect in such works as Raoul de Houdenc's *Songe d'Enfer*, the *Voie de Paradis*, Huon de Méry's *Tournoiement d'Antécrist*, the *Tournoiement d'Enfer* and Jehan de la Motte's fourteenth-century *Voie d'Enfer*. As these titles show, the fear of hell and the devil remains a motivating one, under-lying the increasing penitential motif. The later thirteenth century sees the verse sermon sometimes developing into a full-scale treatise on Repentance addressed to the laity; such is Jehan de Journy's *Disme de Penitence*. Thus the verse sermon comes more and more to reflect the preoccupation with the Sacrament of penitence; and with Nicholas Bozon we may see the mature working-out of this theme, along a number of parallel lines of development.

One pertinent practical question remains: one may usefully accept the term 'verse sermon' in a discussion of the genre, but does this give one the right to assume that Bozon's poems were actually preached from the pulpit? Are they in fact the authentic texts of sermons? There is no positive proof. Certainly Bozon himself uses the word 'sermon', and in its preaching context: in his third poem he states *Ly sage prestre ben le freyt / Ke ceste chose en sarmoun deyt* (vv. 27-28), and he concludes his seventh text: *Pryez Deu pur Bosoune / Ke vous fet ceo sarmoun* (vv. 71-72). This is a prayer-ending typical of medieval preached sermons in Latin and the vernacular, and may be found again in the opening piece: *Jeo pri Deu ke seum prest / A vostre venue, si ly plet* (vv. 115-16), in the second: *Hore deyt prier li Bosouns . . . / Ke a cele joye Deu nous meyne* (vv. 193, 196), and in the fifth: *Deu nus doynt issy merir / Ke nous pussum a ly venyr* (vv. 69-70). Similarly, a direct address to the preacher's audience is heard throughout the texts: *Si vous plest a mey entendre / La resoun pur quey powez aprendre* (IV, 35-36), *Hore escotez ke jeo vus die / Ke cest ensaumple sygnefie* (V, 31-32), *Pur ceo, seygnurs, enpensez / Ke poy de temps ycy avez* (V, 55-56), *Escotez, seygnours, escotez* (VI, 1), *Hore escotez e vous dirrai* (VII, 1), *Pur ceo, seygnurs, laÿs e clers / Ke avez oÿ ceo quatre vers* (IX, 81-82). Admittedly, this conventional rhetoric does not automatically imply that the text itself was delivered from the pulpit: one may equally cite the incipit of another Anglo-Norman poem, *Oyez, seignurs, sermun / Ne orrez si veir nun*, which goes on for almost two thousand lines in tailed stanzas.[34] However, Bozon's themes are sermon themes, and the very first text has as its precise subject

---

[34] E. Langfors, *Les incipit des poèmes français antérieurs au XVIe siècle* (Paris, 1917), p. 244; *Le Roman des romans et Le sermon en vers*, edited by F. J. Tanquerey (Paris, 1922): the poet insists that *Cest sermun est dist / Pur vus e escrit* (vv. 1903-04), and urges people to read it often.

the preacher and his sermon. One may at least suppose with some confidence that the matter of each of Bozon's nine poems represents one of the friar's own sermons, turned by him into the various verse-forms at which he was so adept, just as a number of the exempla in his *Contes moralisés* bear the signs of his personal preaching style.

MANUSCRIPT AND TEXT

British Library MS Additional 46919 is a reasonably thick tome of 211 folios, but of modest format (23 cm X 17 cm) – as are many manuscripts of Franciscan origin destined for practical use and consultation, almost as 'pocket-books'. It has recently (1965) been rebound in plain mid-brown leather, and provided with a functional slip-case. The only decoration is afforded by the title on the spine in gold-tooling: *Herebert Collection*. In fact the presence of this manuscript on the shelves of the British Library is comparatively recent: it was more traditionally known among previous generations of scholars as 'Phillipps MS 8336', having once been one of the more celebrated items in the vast Cheltenham collection of Sir Thomas Phillipps. It had earlier formed part of the collection of Richard Heber who had purchased it from a William Fermour of Tusmore (Oxon.), a descendant of Henry Farmer of Tusmore who is credited with its possession in 1697 by Bernard's *Catalogi librorum manuscriptorum Angliae et Hiberniae.*[1]

The manuscript is one of the great single sourcebooks of Anglo-Norman religious verse, and in particular of the works of Nicholas Bozon. It contains his *Contes moralisés*, the *Plainte d'Amour, Le Char d'Orgueil*, his two allegorical Passion poems, the nine Verse Sermons, the poem on 'Denaturesse', the *Desputeyson du cors et de l'alme*, the two texts for and against women, and various poems devoted to the Virgin. The manuscript also offers other devotional poems, an Invocation to the Cross, a *Débat de la Vierge et de la Croix*, an Address by Christ crucified to Sinners, a finely ambiguous poem on True (Christian) Love, a witty but improving Debate between mother and daughter on the choice of a husband, an allegorical pastiche of a Devil's Pact (*La Lettre du Prince des Envieux*, also found in the compendious *Lumere as Lais*), a catechismal allegory *Le Chastel de leal amour*, Thibaut d'Amiens's *Priere Nostre-Dame*, Simund de Freine's *Roman de Philosophie*, and a popular moralising poem on worldliness and repentance known as the *Pleure-chante*. There are other texts: Hue de Tabarie's *Ordre de Chevalerie*, a collection of proverbs, Walter de Bibbesworth's celebrated verse Treatise on the French Language, Twiti's *Art de Venerie*, an anonymous essay on falconry, Latin notes (with French glosses) on

[1] Meyer, 'Notice et extraits . . .', pp. 497–500; the latest account of the manuscript is found in *Catalogue No. 79* of W. H. Robinson, Pall Mall (London, 1950), pp.. v–vi.

falconry and tournament terminology and equipment, and a letter describing a good hawk. There is a prose treatise on asceticism, and also a number of culinary recipes. . . .

From this list it can be seen that the works preserved by the manuscript are all devotional, allegorical, didactic or of a generally instructive nature: a mass of most useful material, ideal grist for the mill of the Franciscan preacher; they extend over thirteen quires, all copied in the early part of the fourteenth century by up to a dozen hands. The manuscript is known to have been in the possession of — and most likely put together by — Friar William Herebert, lector in Divinity to the Franciscans at Oxford and, as already mentioned, a noted preacher and poet in his own right. The manuscript's final bunch of folios contains three of Herebert's hellfire Latin sermons, and also a number of very polished divine lyrics in English, translated by him from Latin hymns and written out in his own hand.[2] Herebert's interest in the earlier contents of his book is evidenced by his frequent marginal annotations to texts and poems that particularly catch his eye; these inevitably include some of Bozon's works, and Herebert has been so taken with the eighth Verse Sermon that he translates it into an English carol, with the same verse-form: this is in fact the only Anglo-Norman text known to have been translated by Herebert, and testifies to the master's appreciation of his fellow-friar.

Bozon's Verse Sermons are found in a continuous set of nine, written as prose (with punctuation-marks normally indicating the verse-form) and each with its own introductory rubric in the form of a jingling theme-couplet, on fols 80^r-85^v, the last folio being the final leaf of the seventh quire. The initial sermon follows straight on from the previous text, the anonymous *Débat de la Vierge et de la Croix*; there is here no attribution to the poet, but the second sermon contains the lines *Hore deyt prier li Bosouns / pur ly e autre conpaingnouns* (fol. 82^r); and the seventh concludes (fol. 84^r) with the couplet *Pryez Deu pur Bosoune / ke vous fet ceo sarmoun*. Immediately following the final sermon, fol. 85^v, is a ten-line *Ave* by Bozon (*Jeo vous salu, reyne de mercy e de pyté* . . .), rounded off by a second *Ave* in two tailed couplets. The rest of the leaf is blank. The nine sermons are copied by the same hand in a square English script typical of many Anglo-Norman manuscripts of the early fourteenth century. The rubric titles are written in red, with faint guidewords in black observable in the margin; initial capitals throughout the texts, two

---

[2] This is stated on fol. 205^r: 'Istos hympnos et antiphonas quasi omnes et cetera transtulit in anglicum, non semper de verbo ad verbum, sed frequenter sensum aut non multum declinando, et etiam manu sua scripsit frater Willelmus Herebert'. Herebert's English version of Bozon's eighth Sermon is found on fols 208^v-209^r.

lines tall, are missing, but the left-hand margin contains the appropriate guide-letter.

As for the date of composition, the texts appear to be closely contemporary with the manuscript, as they have much in common with the *Contes moralisés* that are products of Bozon's later career. An exception, however, is the penultimate sermon which, it will be shown, on the evidence of further manuscripts is to be considered one of Bozon's earlier lyric works, of late thirteenth-century date, and subsequently remodelled to fit into the sermon-series. The two other manuscripts (MS Lambeth Palace Library 522 and British Library MS Sloane 1611) that contain the variants of this eighth sermon will be described subsequently, in the relevant chapter.

In the study of the sermons that follows, the text quoted from manuscript is conserved as far as possible with the minimum of emendations; most concern the omission of individual letters. In two or three cases, where the copyist is more seriously at fault, the suggested corrections (contained within square brackets) are explained in footnotes.

NICHOLAS BOZON'S NINE VERSE SERMONS

The verses that go to make up these multi-faceted sermons reveal all Bozon's skill in preaching the essential Franciscan message crisply, trenchantly and with striking imagery. An inevitable theme linking all the poems together is that of repentance: man the sinner is urged to show a proper contrition for his earthly misdeeds, and thus avoid the gaping maw of Hell and eternal damnation. God is shown as proffering salvation, which only human 'desmesure' puts in jeopardy. Running through the sermons like a pack of wild dogs are the sins of Arrogance, Greed, Envy and Hypocrisy — those faults attacked again and again in the moralising literature of the Middle Ages. To counter them Bozon proposes the great Franciscan virtues of modesty, humility, poverty and a contrite spirit, all contributing to his concept of *bone vie* to which he returns over and again.

These poems give us a most vivid picture of the medieval Friar at work, preaching to the people, to the bilingual classes in England at the turn of the fourteenth century. Indeed, through Bozon's verses we become as aware of the congregation as of the preacher and his sermon, for our poet has the wit and the ability to portray with sometimes merciless accuracy the human types he sees before him from his poetic pulpit: young and old, essentially materialistic middle-class townsfolk who yawn and look away when they should be weeping and looking into their hearts. It is Bozon's highly personal assault on such people that adds spice to his sermons: we can see him pointing his finger at such-a-one or such-a-one, and hear him naming names, and holding up their shortcomings to general mockery, and the improvement of their souls.

The nine sermons are as follows, as introduced by their manuscript-rubrics:

(1) *La parole Deu ke est preché*
   a rai de solail est cumparee.
— one hundred and sixteen lines lines varying from six to twelve syllables, but predominantly octosyllabic, in rhyming couplets with some monorhyming (vv. 21-26, 73-80, 91-98, 99-102, 109-14). Fols 80^r-81^r.

(2) *Peynes e joies cy lisez*
   k'en l'autre vie serrunt trovez.
— thirty-three stanzas of double tailed-couplets (aabccb): octosyllabic, with tails of half-line four syllables. Fols 81^r-82^r.

(3) *Ke fous funt a seynz moleste*
ke meynent treche par jour de feste.
— thirty lines, in octosyllabic rhyming couplets. Fol. 82^r.

(4) *Coment nous sumus si contrarious*
a nostre seygnur k'est sy dous.
— four monorhymed stanzas, the first three of twelve lines, basically octosyllabic, and the last of sixteen with a parallel expansion of the metre into decasyllables (5 + 5). Fol. 82^r-82^v.

(5) *Coumparisoun al haust de ceste vie.* (the one rubric not a couplet)
— seventy lines, in octosyllabic rhyming couplets. Fols 82^v-83^r.

(6) *Une courte ditee*
de longe folie usee.
— forty-three lines, in octosyllabic rhyming couplets (the uneven number of lines does not necessarily indicate a lacuna, but is explained by one triplet among the couplets (vv. 7-9). Fol. 83^r-83^v.

(7) *Coment les fole genz*
Se affient trop en testamenz.
— seventy-two lines, in octosyllabic rhyming couplets. Fols 83^v-84^r.

(8) *Vous purveez en ceste vie*
de soustenaunce en l'autre vie.
— Twelve stanzas of double tailed-couplets followed by a tailed-couplet as refrain (aabccb/ddb). Fol. 84^r-84^v. The earlier variants of this text have only ten stanzas.

(9) *Ke plusours unt aÿe*
par un homme de bone vie.
— one hundred and seven lines in octosyllabic rhyming couplets, although a number of successive lines are monorhymed, effectively hiding the discrepancy (which may in any case be due to a degree of scribal error, vv. 14-15). Fols 84^v-85^v.

At this point one may note Bozon's achievement in varying the patterns of his sermons, not merely from tiny *boutade* to sustained poems of 200 lines, but also from the narrative couplet norm into monorhyme and into the lyrical tail-rhyme that he employs to great effect elsewhere in his verses (notably in his *Plainte d'Amour*). The use of tail-rhyme is a marked feature of Anglo-Norman divine and didactic poetry, owing much to Latin originals (and possibly to a Franciscan predilection for the form, as much of the verse is found in Franciscan manuscript collections), and running parallel in the fourteenth century with similar forms in the ME lyric. A further, unmistakably Anglo-Norman feature of Bozon's verse is the highly flexible metre, under the English influence of a strong expiratory stress; hence the 'Anglo-Norman octosyllable' — or rather a marriage of hepta-syllables and octosyllables — and a similar degree of tolerance around the decasyllable. Far from being a debased offshoot of a pure continental original (and one should beware of assuming any such 'pure original' in OF verse), Anglo-Norman versification is a working system in its own right, with its own vigour and effect amply illustrated by Bozon's poetry.

THE FIRST SERMON:
ON PREACHERS AND SUNRAYS

*La parole Ḍeu ke est preché
a rai de solail est cumparee.*

The opening poem of the sequence is perhaps the most personal of all,
since with its titular likening of sermons to sunrays it becomes in effect an
apt and telling 'Apology for the Preacher', the argument being clinched by
an idiosyncratic conceit typical of Bozon.

A brief introduction urges man to accept the Word of God, in sermons,
comparing the soul deprived of instruction to a body starved of food, and
becoming most feeble:

Ben deit home ke alme porte,
Ke sanz aprise la portereit morte,
Receyvere e tenir en esperit
La parole Deu ho grant delit.
Le cors serreit en bref tens mort
Si par viaunde ne huzt cumfort,
E alme cherreit en grand languor
Si par aprise ne hut socour.

4

8

— as a good educated friar, Bozon sets great store in his works by the
efficacy of *aprise*: the learning of the correct way of behaviour. Having
made this essential point he swings into action, looks about him and
pillories the *juvenceus* in his audience: the young gallants, the 'jeunesse
dorée' whose beauty is all too soon to fade, like a fine flower. These are
for him classic examples of wilful sinners, refusing to heed his sermon or
to gain instruction from it. He lets them condemn themselves and their
pleasure-loving frivolity out of their own mouths; they feel beset by
preachers, and would dearly wish the friars to turn into huntsmen and thus
be of use to them in their sport:

Hore wount disaunt li juvenceus
Ke coyntes sunt, jolifs e beus,
La ki beauté resemble la flour
Ke matyn verdoy, au vespre gette colour:
'Nous awoum' funt il 'trop de precheours!
Nous vodrum meuz ke fussent venours
E nus heidis[e]nt au boys chacer,

12

16   Ke tant nus venissent sovent precher.
    [Usum] le secle tant cum dure:
    De luy sarmoun ne preygnoum ja cure!'

— Bozon criticises man's youthful folly in very similar terms in his *Contes moralisés*, drawing a Scriptural derivation:

. . . Puis si prent le vert chimyn, ceo est jolitee en juvente, com font les enfauntz, en qi noun dit l'escripture: 'Usoms le siecle tant com dure nostre juvente' *Utamur creatura tanquam in juventate celeriter.*[1]

For all their general popularity, the wandering friars must many times have seen their sermons fall on such stony ground, and moralising texts are quick to condemn an excessive addiction to hunting. Sermon-shunners are not unique individuals; and Jacques de Vitry, in his *Sermones vulgares* and in the context of the preacher's vital mission to win souls, tells somewhat ruefully of a man, held back by the crowd in church and so unable to escape the preacher, praying for the same deliverance from this sermon that he has already had from a hundred others.[2]

The youths' *desmesure* increases: they condemn all preachers as horrid spoilsports, forever burdening their hearts, forbidding their pleasures, castigating their sins and making the world a poorer place for their preaching:

    'Il funt nos quers a malhese;
20   Ne wuille Deus ke ceo nus plese:
    Il nous defendent nos joliftez,
    E nous rehercent nos pecchez.
    Li secle est hore mout enpireez
24   Pus ke precheours nous hunt prechez . . .'

— indeed, the friars' very attacks on sin breed more sin, putting ideas into folk's minds:

    'Nous trovem hore plus de pecché
    Ke avaunt lur venue furent pensez.'

— a similar example of the perverse obduracy of young Philistines is provided, again, by Jacques de Vitry, in a personal reminiscence: he once

---

[1] See the edition by P. Meyer and L. Toulmin Smith, p. 43; the reference is to the Vulgate version of Wisdom of Solomon II. 6. In the MS of our sermon the scribe has in fact written *Lhussem*, in possible confusion with 'Lessum' ('laisser le siecle'); the correction has been made from the example quoted above of the OF phrase 'user le siecle', in this context surely the original choice.

[2] See the edition by Crane, p. 59. The *Tabula exemplorum* more savagely likens such sermon-haters to scuttling toads: 'sunt similes bufonibus, qui exeunt vineas cum florent; sic quidam cum predicari incipitur, exeunt ecclesiam . . .' (see the edition by Welter, p. 66).

confessed some youths who had vandalised fields and stolen grapes; they promised glibly to mend their ways, but on leaving the church they noticed some more vineyards, and with much yelling rushed upon the grapes again.[3]

At this point Bozon cuts short his opposition with a threatening word; these young fools will suffer bitterly when death lays them low:

<blockquote>

	Ceo dient les fous, e lur peisera
28	Kant la mort les assaudera;
	Ke jeo les fray la moustreysoun
	Ke pecché ne veent mye par sarmoun,
	Mes par sarmoun (fol. 80^v) est aparceu
32	Le peril de pecché e meuz conu.

</blockquote>

— in order to prove that preaching reveals sin and does not cause it, he embarks upon the *exemplum* that will become the key to the sermon. He selects the everyday image of the sun shining through a window into a room and catching the dust in the air; normally, the tiny particles of dust (*attonies*) are invisible to the naked eye, however hard one looks; and yet they are there, like minute crumbs, and they are perceived through sunlight:

<blockquote>

	La ray du solail kant est entré
	Sale ou chambre fenestree,
	La put l'em ver la poudrere
36	En ray du solail par lumere.
	De costé ne verrez nule ren,
	Ja ne avisez vous si ben,
	E si volent les attonies
40	De tote parz cum fussent mies;
	Mes il vous peerent soulement
	En rai du solail apertement.

</blockquote>

— who would claim that a ray of light actually brings dust into a room? No-one: it but reveals the dust flying about in the atmosphere:

<blockquote>

	Quideus pur ceo ke rai du solail
44	Vous eit amené poudre ou pail?
	Nai! ceo sachez de veritee;
	Mes par le solail vus est moustree
	Hou la poudre en meisun vole.

</blockquote>

— and thus with direct and trenchant rhetoric Bozon explains his example:

[3] Ibid., p. 126.

48   Ausy est de seynt escole:
            Si vous avisez ben la chose,
            Vous troverez veyrs la parclose.
            Pecché comenza mout par temps
52   De multeplier entre gens,
            E par defaute de seynte aprise
            Si n'i out il nule devise
            Entre peril e surtee,
56   Entre pecché e bountee.

— the dust is sin, multiplying in this world, but invisibly; and without
the benefit of that crucial, holy and eye-opening instruction none can distinguish the gap between right and wrong, mortal peril and salvation.
Christ, however, is the sun, and preachers are, precisely, those rays of light
sent by him out into the world to illuminate the dark hearts of men and to
enable them to see clearly by means of their instructive sermons the host
of sins hitherto concealed and invisible in the darkness:

            Mes kant ly solail ses rays getoit,
            Ly douz Jhesu, ke enveoyt
            Par tote teres ses precheours
60   A gens ke hurent les quers oscurs,
            Lors pot l'em ver par clareté
            De seynte aprise la verité,
            De menuz pecchez apparisaunz
64   Ke en orbisouns tapirent avant.

— this is a good enough resumé of the Franciscan mission to the people;
the role of the preacher is indeed stressed in the Exempla-collections, in
various signal images: for Jacques de Vitry, the preacher is God's bell;[4]
while the *Tabula exemplorum* prefers a Bestiary-list, likening him successively to a sheep giving fine milk, to a high-flying eagle and to a lion.[5]
   The initial exposition over, Bozon is now able to give the lie to the
young good-for-nothings who believe that sermons beget sin:

            Lors ne quid pas ke seit resoun
            De dire ke pecché crest par sarmoun,
            Mes ke sarmoun par sa lumere
68   Nous eyt moustree la poudrere.

— and he enthusiastically pursues his chosen metaphor: having already

---

   [4] *Sermones vulgares*, edited by Crane, p. 62 (no. CXXXIX).
   [5] See the edition by Welter, pp. 64–65.

conveyed the telling idea of man's sins lurking treacherously in the dark, he goes on to warn his (by now more attentive) listener that if he continues to close the window to his heart and so bar God's word, then sin will breed within, all unseen and unsuspected, like some deadly germ, of which the very minutest particle is enough to assault and taint the soul, and drag it down hideously at the moment of death:

> Fermez la fenestre de toun quer,
> Ke parole de Deu ne pusse entrer,
> E pecché sourdra de jour en jour
> 72   Ke ne est parceu en tenebrur,
> E ren ne verrez ke vous greve;
> Mes ja le meyns le pecché leve
> E fet l'alme orde e bleve,
> 76   E kant le quer par mort se creve
> La chose ke avant apparut sueve
> Lors appara hidouse e greve;
> E pur folie curte e breve
> 80   La pey ne durra ke ja ne cheve.

Thus are men deceived and condemned without respite by their brief, sinning pleasures; and the preacher moves towards his necessary and detailed exhortation: he urges his flock to recognise their sins through God's sunrays, to make due amends and to prepare themselves fittingly for death. As a friar sworn to holy poverty and preaching to a materialistic and well-to-do congregation, he very appropriately recommends the great medieval social and improving virtue of generosity as a proper expiation, in the form of alms and offerings:

> Doun est dounk saunz nul fail
> De regarder le ray du solail,
> La parole Deu, ke nous aprent
> 84   De ver noz pecchez apertement,
> Ke fere pussum les amendes
> Par aumoune e par offrendes,
> E pur tutes aventures
> 88   Seum prestes totes houres;
> Kar la mort nous fet somouns
> Ke touz jours seum prodeshommes.

— it is a key tenet of medieval thought, stimulated by an often brutal reality, that death comes all too soon to sweep away earthly vanity; that is a telling incentive for people always to be *prodeshommes*. Like his congregation and his age, Bozon is much possessed by death; and the final portion of his sermon develops logically into a very fine evocation of the Triumph, of the terrible destruction to be feared by all. Man cannot struggle against death, and anyone who forgets his mortality will groan bitterly when the time comes. The wise man is he who has no need to quake at death's approach:

	Cil est hony ke mort ne creent,
92	E a ses somouns pre[s]t ne veent;
	Kar trestouz morir nous cov[e]nt:
	De countre estrivere ne vaut neent.
	Ke en sa vie de mort ne sovent,
96	Kant mort se moustre, forment geent;
	Dounk cyl est sage ke la se teent
	Hou douter ne estut kant mort s'en veent.
	Mort est laroun ke tot atrape,
100	De mort la meyn tut agrape,
	Mort (fol. 81ʳ) nous fet de tere chape
	E tout a riche kaun[k']il hape.

— death's hand clutches all, death grants us a cloak of earth, death seizes the rich man's ill-gotten gains. This is a dramatic and Villonesque picture, in some contrast to the rather calmer definitions offered by the earlier Franciscan exempla-collections. The *Tabula exemplorum* likens death to an arrow: 'mors est sagitta domini . . .';[6] while the *Speculum laicorum* chooses a set of Biblical-cum-Classical images: 'mors . . . est eternus sompnus, dissolucio corporis, divitum pavor, pauperum desiderium, inevitabilis eventus, incerta peregrinacio . . .'.[7] Bozon's inspiration here is clearly Hélinant de Froidmont's *Vers de la Mort*; indeed, vv. 99–102 are taken almost word for word from among the celebrated list of Death's activities in stanzas XXXI and XXXII of Hélinant's powerful work.[8] Desiring to shock his audience to the full, however, Bozon has changed the original 'Morz est la roiz' (death is a net, a trap) to something even more

---

[6] See the edition by Welter, p. 49.

[7] See the edition by Welter, pp. 76–77.

[8] Edited by F. Wulff and E. Walberg (Paris, SATF, 1895), pp. 28–30; v. 91 also corresponds to XXXIV, 1 (p. 31). Hélinant's influence was considerable; elsewhere in Anglo-Norman literature frequent borrowings from the *Vers de la Mort* are found in an anonymous thirteenth-century *Poème sur l'amour de Dieu et la haine du péché* (edited by P. Meyer in *Romania*, 29 (1900), pp. 5–21), much of which was later incorporated into some MSS of the *Manuel des Péchés*, c. 1260 (see E. J. Arnould, *Le Manuel des Péchés: étude de littérature religieuse anglo-normande* (Paris, 1940), pp. 205–21). Bozon would thus have had Hélinant's verses easily to hand, in one form or another.

violent; death is now described as a *laroun*: a brigand lying in wait for his victims. The sermon's conclusion continues to draw directly, but with skilful compression, from Hélinant; Bozon combines vv. XXIX, 1-2 and XXVIII, 1-2 of the *Vers de la Mort* to form a brief traditional 'Ubi sunt' motif, in order to bring home once and for all the essential message of the vanity of worldly delights and fineries, of which the gilded *juvenceus* that have provoked the sermon are such clear representatives:

	Quey vaut honour ou richesce?
104	Key vaut beauté hou hautesce?
	Kanke travail en lounge tens cret,
	Mort a un houre tut defet.

The sermon ends, as all good sermons should, on an even more dramatic climax, as Bozon turns to address Death personified, and bids him warn his fellow-mortals that they have less time than they think before his inexorable approach; the final image is the chilling folk-symbol of Death the Hunter, here positively welcomed by Bozon[9] as a means of instilling in all a salutary fear that will purge their hearts of the filth of sin. Bozon includes himself in the number, and concludes his sermon with a prayer that they may all be ready to face death, with God's grace. For this ending he rearranges and inserts some of Hélinant's opening lines, his vv. 107 and 111-13 corresponding to IV. 1, 8 and 10-11 of the *Vers de la Mort*:[10]

	Mort, fay garnir mes amys
108	Ke par tey ne seyent souzpris:
	Dy lur ke il unt meyns de espace
	Ke escrit ne truvent en lur face.
	Tu ke juhes a la chace,
112	Grant ben fes par ta manace:
	Ke pour de tey nus purge e sace
	De meynt ordure ke quer purchace.
	Jeo pri Deu ke seum prest
116	A vostre venue, si ly plet. AMEN

This initial sermon already reveals one of the most striking features of Nicholas Bozon's poetry: the very Franciscan weaving into his sermons of highly concrete and practical examples in order to make and the better to

---

[9] In another context, in his *Contes moralisés*, it is the devil that Bozon chooses to dress in huntsman's clothes and send out, with a pack of allegorical hounds, in search of sinners (edited by Meyer and Toulmin Smith, pp. 29-37: 'Quod diabolus venatur animas canibus suis maledictus' — an exemplium subsequently found in the *Gesta Romanorum*).

[10] See the edition by Wulff and Walberg, pp. 4-5.

illustrate basic didactic points. Here, the characterisation (all too recognisable) of the wanton and intolerant youths is followed by the sustained image of the sun's rays and the dusty room. There is, however, an added complexity in Bozon's work: and one should note his ability to blend together a mundane item and a highly intellectual conceit. There is indeed a deeper *senefiance* in a sunray: the metaphysical association of light and the Godhead is an important one in medieval religious philosophy, and had been notably acclaimed in the first half of the twelfth century by Suger, abbot of St-Denis. Suger's new Gothic basilica, with its stone columns rising up to meet the coloured light in the windows, which in turn streamed down to illuminate the sanctuary and to catch the inset precious stones of the 'trésor' carefully displayed along the High Altar, was a joint product of technology and philosophy, and proved vital to the development of medieval church architecture. In describing Christ as the sun, and in fashioning his example around the saving rays, Bozon follows in this tradition of light metaphysics; but he also combines it with a further element, an almost clinical detailing of the microscopic *attonies*, the tiny dust-particles in the air rendered visible through the medium of intense light. This passage may well owe something to the influence among the Franciscan community of Robert Grosseteste and his celebrated treatise on Optics.[11] Between 1229 and 1235, before becoming Bishop of Lincoln, Grosseteste was lector to the Franciscan school at Oxford, devoting some time to the study of optics and the properties of the rainbow; the great philosopher Roger Bacon was one of many friars influenced by his teachings on the metaphysics of light.

Grosseteste considered light to be the primal corporeal form; there existed for him a universal continuum: as light flowed from the sun down through the air, so there flowed an animal essence (*vis*) through man's own body, stemming from his rational *virtus* (this concept was derived from early neo-Platonic sources, via the Jewish philosopher Avicebron). Thus for Grosseteste the study of optics would prove the key to the understanding of the physical world, and he expressed his scientific theories in three main works: *De Colore, De Lineis* and *De Iride*. In these he tackled the problems of reflection and refraction, and so the part played by light and optics in magnification: '. . . it may be possible for us to read the smallest letters at incredible distances, or to count sand, or grains, or seeds, or any sort of minute objects'.[12] There is a fair resemblance between this excerpt from *De Iride* and Bozon's *poudrere* and *attonies*.

[11] The standard work on Grosseteste's scientific writings is A. C. Crombie, *Robert Grosseteste and the Origins of Experimental Science* (Oxford, 1953); his theories on light are discussed at pp. 104-34.

[12] Ibid., p. 119. The general commentary on the revealing properties of light may be traced back to Seneca, *Naturales quaestiones*, Book I: 'De ignibus in aere'.

A second connection with Grosseteste is perhaps more explicit. Bozon has extended his metaphor and likened the sunrays to preachers and their sermons; in his celebrated letter of recommendation to Pope Gregory IX composed around 1238, Robert Grosseteste praises the English Franciscans, stressing their zeal, their example and their preaching mission:

> . . . Illuminant enim totam nostram regionem praeclara luce praedicationis et doctrinae . . . [13]

— the friars illuminate the land with the bright light of their preaching and teaching. Bozon seems to have taken this proudly to heart and used the image as the text for his own sermon, elaborating it with metaphysical and optical details to be found in Grosseteste's other writings.

In his *Contes moralisés* Bozon quotes a specific example of the enlightening effect of a preacher's sermon on a hardened sinner with an *alme mout hidous*, who for once did not seek to leave the church beforehand:

> . . . Celui demora od les autres a mouster tant qe parole Dieux fust prechee, e par cel sermoun conceut en queor graund repentaunce de ces maux, e out ferme volenté de confesser . . . [14]

— he clearly hopes by his own sermon to instil a similar timely change of heart in his congregation, even among the *juvenceus*.

In this first text, Nicholas Bozon has begun with carefree living and ended, with grim irony, with Death. In his second poem he takes the logical step beyond death, to deal with the soul's fate.

[13] *Epistolae*, edited by H. Luard, p. 180.
[14] *De confessione et contricione*, edited by Meyer and Toulmin Smith, p. 82.

THE SECOND SERMON:
THE TWIN BANQUETS

Peynes e joies cy lisez
k'en l'autre vie serrunt trovez

This sermon is the most substantial, and the most forcefully allegorical, of the nine texts. As the rubric indicates, Bozon is here taking up the theme of Heaven and Hell which medieval iconography develops into such a powerful example of antithetical parallelism. The great Last Judgement portals of the twelfth and thirteenth centuries (Vézelay, Autun, Reims, Bourges, and so on throughout western Christendom) present the awesome figures of Christ Judge and of St Michael weighing the souls that either flock joyously to his right to be received into Abraham's bosom and the company of Heaven, or troop off left screaming, goaded by demons, to be pitched into the cauldron bubbling in the fires of Hell's mouth. The scene is taken up in stained glass, in medieval drama and in moralising literature, and is aimed, like some horrific object-lesson, straight at the hearts and souls of the people, of whom François Villon's aged mother is a famous example:

> ... Au moustier voy dont suis paroissienne
> Paradis paint, ou sont harpes et lus,
> Et ung enfer ou dampnez sont boullus:
> L'ung me fait paour, l'autre joye et liesse ...[1]

Bozon's sermon is thus literally a 'hellfire' one, warning the unrepentant sinners in his audience of the terrible dangers they are courting. He has, however, chosen a somewhat unusual treatment: instead of describing salvation and damnation in traditional iconographical detail, or else borrowing from the Psychomachia to tell of a straightforward battle between Good and Evil, he has visualised the Last Judgement in more practical social terms, of two puissant allegorical lords holding two very contrasting feasts for their respective vassals:

> I   Ben e Mal unt fet covenant
>   Ke checun fra feste grant
>   A ses amis:
> 4   Mes il y averunt diversitez

[1] *Testament*, vv. 895–98, edited by A. Longnon (Paris, CFMA [4ᵉ éd./Nouv. tirage], 1970).

> A les festes ke sunt criez
> En divers païs.

Bozon's imagery is drawn from the niceties of medieval hospitality and table-etiquette; 'Mal' is the first to summon his guests, mortal sinners of both high and low degree, and to bestow upon them all the dubious pleasures of his hell-house, where they will suffer everlasting torments, with neither wine nor beer to slake their terrible thirst:

	II	Mal ad somouns touz les mauveis
8		Haut e bas ke tenent leys
		De pecché mortel
		En puz de enfern mut parfunt:
		Ky la venent arivé sunt
12		A mal hostel.
	III	Kar il averunt feym e seyf,
		Si ne troverent ke die: 'Beyf',
		Vin ne serveyse;
16		Touz jours criunt e crierunt
		E lur peynes touz jours durount
		A lounge teyse.

— the stanzas that follow are full of inventive force as Bozon reveals the sorry plight of these guests in Hell, seated at a table of bitterness and regaled by one grisly course after another. The basic motif of the Infernal Feast is not original; in his *Songe d'Enfer* the early thirteenth-century poet Raoul de Houdenc has Beelzebub sit down with his retinue to a banquet of roasted sinners: squabbling fighters *a l'aillie*, usurers *lardé si cras dessus la coste*, murderers *destrempré as aus*, old over-ripe whores, heretics *en broche de fer*, hypocritical nuns *au cretonné* and sodomites *bien cuiz en honte*, the whole washed down with *vilonies en leu de vin*.[2] The contemporary *Voie de Paradis* has the narrator moving rather repetitively from one allegorical hostel to another: from Contrition, where

> . . . Moult a mengier et moult a boire
> Eumes nous en sa meson.
> Seglous eumes a foison:
> Angoisses et lermes beumes . . .[3]

---

[2] Edited by P. Lebesgue (Paris, 1908), vv. 422–604; cf. also J. Frappier, 'Châtiments infernaux et peur du diable', *Cahiers de l'Association internationale des études françaises*, 3–5 (1953), 92–94.

[3] Edited by P. Lebesgue (appendix to above edition), vv. 193–96.

— to Love of God where is provided the best in food and drink.[4] Finally, Huon de Méry's *Tournoiement Antecrist*[5] (c. 1232), partly inspired by the *Songe d'Enfer*, contains, at vv. 408-79, a spirited description of an infernal feast set before the knights of Antichrist and including *une merveilleuse friture | De pechiez*.

This last allegorical conceit: the sinners being the eaters rather than the eaten, is the one adopted by Bozon, who here provides the most lavish and sustained description of all. He pays great attention to accurate detail, so that behind the Devil's meal, with its allegorical horrors full of worms and venom, we may see a clear account of an early fourteenth-century banquet. First, the basic side-servings of wine, bread and piquant sauce:

IV	En lu de payn lur est donee
20	Vil reproche de lur pecché
	Par corouze;
	Soufre e venym est lur beyvere,
	E feel de dragoun pur sause de peyvere
24	A trestouz.

Before the starving sinners, on the foul cloth of Lost Joy, is now served a soup of bitterness at the thought of others' bliss, a verminous meat-course, and an entremets of the Certainty of Doom:

V	Lur vile nape est remenbraunce
	De joie perdue sanz recoverance,
	Ke Deu ne verrount;
28	E lur potage trop est amer
	Ke les autres de sy leger
	Sauvez serrount.

VI	Pur grose char les vermes y sunt,
32	Ke touz jours vivent e viverunt
	A lur nusaunce;
	L'autre mes est certeyneté
	Ke jammés ne averount suaté
36	De allegaunce.

— the meal continues with a third course of blasphemous despair, and concludes with wretched cheese and fruit:

VII	Le terce mees est maluree
	Ke touz jours maudient Dampnedee
	En desperaunce.

[4] Ibid., vv. 790-808.   [5] Edited by G. Wimmer (Marburg, 1888).

40   En lu de fornage il unt tristour,
                En lu de frut, graunt horrour
                    De lur semblaunce.

There follow hellish travesties of medieval etiquette, of the social con-
ventions of after-dinner water-basins and warm towels (tears and burning
impatience), spiced sweetmeats (noisome stenches), harping and minstrel-
entertainment in the hall (plucked consciences and condemned men's
groans); while curses take the place of Grace:

VIII   Tut sanz laver beyvent lennes,
44   En lu de tualle, lunge tennes
                    De impacience;
               En lu d'especes, grant puyné,
               En lu de harpe, amerté
48   De conscience.

IX   En lu de graces il funt priere
               Ke Dé confunde pere e mere
                  Ke les nourryt;
52   En lu de chaunzoun plurt e geent
               Haut e bas ke la veent,
                  Sanz nul delit.

— and the doomed guests rise from table and are ushered to a round of
icy baths, fiery beds and an eternity of communal darkness:

X   Lur bayn est prest en ewe freyde,
56   Si ne trovent ke lur eyde
                  Tant ne kant.
               Pus sunt cochez en un lit
               Ke tout enviroune un tapit (fol. 81ᵛ)
60   De fu ardaunt.

XI   Hors du lit enflambee
               Sount mis en ewe engelee
                  De grant freidour;
64   E pus de ewe engelee
               Au lit returnent enbrasee,
                  Maugré lour.

XII   Touz jours sunt en oscureté,
68   Hou ja ne ert jour mes la nutee
                  Ke ja ne fine;

> Cum plus crest lur cumpaygnie,
> Taunt plus averount dure vie
> 72   E plus de puyne.

— the more their numbers swell, the more exquisite becomes their torment. With this Dantesque vision of hell, Bozon reaches the half-way stage of his sermon; he pauses an instant to stress the grim picture of the sinners ensnared for eternity, wishing only for the death that will never come to relieve them:

> XIII   Touz jours vivent sanz morir,
>   E de morir unt grant desir,
>   Ne mourrount pas.
> 76   A male houre fut unke nee
>   Ke la est pris par pecché
>   E mis en laz.

— and then, with a sudden antithesis he turns away from the tough and poisonous meat of Hell to offer us a second repast, this time prepared with the culinary skill of Heaven; this dainty fare is served by Grace and Bounty before guests crowned in glory:

> XIV   Mout est la vile feste,
> 80   Ke lour viaunde est trop reste
>   E veninouse:
>   Deu nos meyne al autre feste,[6]
>   Hou la viaunde est ja preste
> 84   Deliciouse;

> XV   Hou atyre a ses amans
>   Par Grace e Bounté, ses deus serwanz,
>   Grant deyntez;
> 88   Hou touz serrount reys e reïgnes
>   De haute coroune par Deu meïnes
>   Corounez.

In order to provide the most dramatic opening possible to this second feast which must not merely counterpoint the Devil's fare, but indeed overwhelm it, Bozon employs a very effective device: he describes the scene initially through the mouth of Christ himself, acting the role of a divine host and chef. His favoured guests, whom he awaits to serve, are not the earlier souls in just torment, but those alone who are properly summoned

---

[6] At this point, in the margin of the MS, William Herebert annotates the poem for future reference: *De festo bonorum.*

as the elect, and who through private or public suffering and through acts
of charity are the more deserving of heavenly reward:

    XVI   Jesu dit: 'Jeo vendrai
    92   E mys amys servirai
                    A lur gré;
                 Jeo ne [a]tenk[7] for mes eliz
                 Ke fussent venuz e assis
    96   E ordinez.

    XVII   'Ky plus avera pur mey suffert,
                 Hou en privee hou en apert,
                    Plus merit;
    100   Ky plus avera de aumoyne fet,
                 Plus y trovera en sun fet
                    Greynur delit'.

– the preacher is naturally at some pains to insist on this cardinal
moralising principle, in his Franciscan campaign against worldliness and
egoism; and he finds further occasion to elaborate upon the theme as each
aspect of the appetising Feast of the Elect is carefully itemised, in detailed
allegory, to represent a feature of the grace and joy of salvation. The setting first of all, with trenchers of Confirmation (freeing them evermore
from the desire to sin) on a pure and unsulliable cloth spread over a table
of Noble Generosity (allowing each to do as he wishes without let or
hindrance):

    XVIII   'En lu de table jeo frai lever
    104   Tant de franchise en leur quer
                    Ke checun fra
                 Ceo k'yl vout saunz respit,
                 Si ne trovera cuntredit
    108   De nuli la.

    XIX   'Lur blaunche nape ert nettee,
                 Ke jammés ne ert enbrouhee
                    Par ordure;
    112   E lur trencheours cunfermement,
                 Ke de peccher ne averunt talent
                    A nul hore'.

The meal now begins – or rather, the promise of the meal, for Bozon's
use of the future tense here has the necessary effect of indicating that these

---

[7] MS *etenk*. The scribe may here have confused the expected *atendre* with *estendre*,
to set (a table), a reading understandable in general context.

are delights to come for those in his audience who eschew sin. For salt
there will be the savour of Gratitude for salvation,[8] and, by cutting contrast,
the Perdition of all enemies will serve as table-knife; then the guests will be
offered the bread of Divine Grace and the sweet wine of Divine Mercy:

XX	'En lu du sel lur dourrai sauwor
116	De mercier lur creatur
	De lur salvacion;
	En lu de coteus lur mousterai
	Ke lur enemis trebucheray
120	En perdicion.
XXI	'En lu de payn lur asserai
	Grez e graces ke lur rendray
	Ke m'ount ameez;
124	Pus si beyverunt grant douzour
	Ke jeo les faz cel honour
	Ke sunt merciez'.

— a splendid soup will be served, of Protection against misadventure,
followed by a first course of the Knowledge of God's power and of all the
blessed. Nothing will be hidden, but each will know the other's estate,
birth, nationality and by what particular grace he is now saved; the hearts
of all will be open to all, as each feels love for the other and is loved in
return:

XXII	'Pus lur dourrai bon potage,
128	Unkes teel en nuly age
	Fu goustee,
	Ke yl averount assuraunce
	Ke ja ne serrount par mechance
132	Mesgrevé.'
XXIII	Lur primer mees ert conusaunce
	De kankes est fet par la pussance
	Dampnedee:
136	Checun savera dount autre est,
	De quey lingnage est dounke estret,
	E hou fu nee:
XXIV	En queu pays e en queu lu,
140	E quele grace i [l] ad hu
	De estre sauvé; ·

<hr>

[8] There is a neat triple pun here involving *sel*, *savor* and *salver*.

                Chescun verra autry quer,
                Checun savera autre amer
144   E estre amee.

These stanzas reveal a very Franciscan feeling for the shared human experience, for the brotherhood of man in Christ Son of Man; and this delicate mysticism will be maintained to the end of the sermon. It is at this point that Bozon takes over the description himself from Jesus; this has the effect of concentrating the preacher's hold over his material and over his audience, to whom he is now speaking directly.

A second course consists of Security; no one will be turned away (*repué*) from the feast for any sin or accident of birth. All will be accounted noble, but the most deserving will rightly receive the most merit; thus Bozon emphasises more and more the justice and harmony of Paradise:

XXV   E pus lur vendra tot aprés
                De douce choce autre mees
                  De bon endreit,
148   Ke nul ne serra repué
                Ne de lingnage ne de pecché,
                  Queys esteyt.

XXVI   Trestouz gentiz serrount la,
152   Mes ky plus deservy a
                  Ky ke seyt,
                Plus ly ert allouhee
                E plus serra prysee
156   A bon dreyt.

Further courses arrive, enabling each soul to share in the other's bliss, in constant comradeship and perpetual joy, in perfect surroundings:

XXVII   Le terce mees est precious,
                Ke endouzit les quers de touz:
                  Ke checun avera (fol. 82ʳ)
160   De autri joie autant delit
                Cum de la souhe, tant ert parfit
                  E tant amera.

XXVIII   Un autre mees lur ert donee,
164   Ke nul ne serra allounné
                  De ses amys;
                Le quart mees plus amyable
                Ke lur joie est pardurable
168   En beu pays.

— this key word 'joy' is redoubled in the next two stanzas, as Bozon reaches the final part of his sermon. OF *joie* conveys a strong meaning of the ecstasy of love; in a non-religious context (in, for instance, a poem of *fin'amor*) it would have positive sexual connotations. Here it is sublimated to translate the no less ecstatic Franciscan bliss of the spirit, a mysticism tempered by Bozon (down-to-earth even in his raptures) as he associates this ultimate delight with the final courses of cheese (bliss so pure that no greater is to be sought) and desert (Grace manifest, granting these fortunate souls eternal joy):

XXIX	Lour formage est bon e tendre,
	Ke nul desire joie grendre
	K'il ne avera:
172	Si nul desirat plus de joie,
	Ne serreit pas parfite joie
	Ceo ke avera.
XXX	Mes checun scet la desert,
176	Dount il rettent grace apert;
	Ceo k'yl unte:
	Cele joye ke touz jours dure —
	Il nasquirent a bon hure
180	En ceo munde.

— evocative though they may be, these stanzas are not artistically among Bozon's best; it is as though the preacher here clashes briefly with the poet, his sermon-rhetoric leading him into repetitive rhymes and strained syntax. Fortunately, his touch is soon recovered as he brings his feast to a triumphant conclusion, with spices proving the Odour of God; the immaculate soul has no need of washing, and moves on directly to a Grace which is very different from the perverted cursings of the damned:

XXXI	En lu de especes, en lu de peyre,
	Yl [unt] odour ke suef fleyre
	Plus ke rose.
184	Ja ne unt mester de laver
	Hou nule ordure put adeser
	Pur nule chose.
XXXII	Mes lur graces ne oblyent poynt,
188	Kar il les dient mut a poynt
	En chantant;
	E lowent Deu, lur creatour,
	Ke les [ad] monstrez teu douzour
192	Ensemblant.

— and with this singing of the Lord's praises, the preacher-poet ends appropriately enough on a reverent note: praying that God send him and his listeners invitations to dine thus at his table, and save them from the Devil's hospitality:

XXXIII	Hore deyt prier li Bosouns
	Pur ly e autre cumpaingnouns
	Devoutement
196	Ke a cele joye Deu nous meyne,
	E de la feste pus de peyne
	Nous defent.
	AMEN.

This sermon shows Bozon revelling in the specialised conceit, in allegory formed around highly practical everyday objects, occupations or happenings. He employs comparable culinary imagery in his satirical *Char d'Orgueil*, in the course of a depiction of Lady Pride's household: the master cook in the kitchens is called 'Mal Usage' and prepares all food to excess; and he is assisted by kitchen-boys who leave dishes unwashed, and who represent society's *pygaceours* — vain young dandies who fail to cleanse their sinning souls. . . .[9] In both cases we see Bozon illustrating his verses in such a way as to strike home into the hearts of his audience, and continuing his feud with the spoiled *juvenceus* of his first Sermon: hence, one suspects, his choice here of allegory making such play with lavish gastronomy and noble hospitality. The friars were quick to condemn gluttonous banqueters, taking as their text Isaiah 28. 8: 'For all tables are full of vomit and filthiness'; the *Tabula exemplorum* sourly comments on some nobles' excessive feasting, warning that they may eat today who will go hungry tomorrow;[10] and a particularly sharp-tongued anonymous English moralist of the fifteenth century attacks 'the lust and delite in etynge':

... And when the likerous mete cometh eche after other in sondry cours, after the manere of service, than mote thei have bourdes, tryfles and janglynges of vanitees for an entremes, and so wasteth the tyme....[11]

— Nicholas Bozon's Feast of the Damned is thus in spirited company.

[9] *Deux poèmes de Nicholas Bozon*, edited by J. Vising (Göteborg, 1919), vv. 529–36.
[10] 'Festum', edited by Welter, p. 25.
[11] Cf. Owst, *Literature and Pulpit* . . . , pp. 447–48.

THE THIRD SERMON:
DANCING DOWN TO HELL

Ke fous funt a seynz moleste
ke meynent treche par jour de feste

More devilish work is, literally, afoot in this tiny sermon, where Bozon
draws upon further practical illustrations of the wayward behaviour of his
congregation. The 'treche' he attacks most vehemently as a foul practice
is the sport of dancing, and in doing so he joins a legion of fellow-moralists.
The medieval pleasure in dancing rounds to the accompaniment of music
and song is fully attested by the popularity of the lyric genre of the *rondet
de carole*, by numerous manuscript illustrations and by frequent references
in *romans courtois*. One may quote by way of brief examples from that
most acute and experienced observer of the thirteenth-century social
scene, Jehan Renart:

> ... Main a main, em pur lor biau cors,
> Devant le tref, en un pré vert,
> Les puceles et li vallet
> Ront la carole commenciee ...[1]

and again:

> ... Aprés mangiers fu grans la tresce
> Par la maison, et les karoles ...[2]

In the eyes of the Church this was seen as indecorous cavorting, particularly when it took the form of public displays of merriment in the streets
and squares on sabbaths and holy-days[3] — of which perhaps the most considerable and notorious demonstration was the Lenten Carnival, or Chari-
vari. It is this that Nicholas Bozon attacks most scathingly in his poem: for
him dancing is indeed the Devil's delight, and in it he sees all the wanton
and heedless worldliness which as a good friar he must ever oppose:

> [E]n escripture awoum trovee
> Ke treche est dreyt apelee

---

[1] *Guillaume de Dole*, edited by F. Lecoy (Paris, CFMA, 1963), vv. 507–10.
[2] *Escoufle*, edited by F. P. Sweetser (Geneva, TLF, 1974), vv. 3651–52.
[3] The *Manuel des Péchés* (edited by F. J. Furnivall in *Robert of Brunne's 'Hand-
lyng Synne'* (London, EETS, 1901, 1903)) tells us, vv. 6931–87, of a mixed group of
dancers who ignore the priest's entreaties to stop and to attend Mass, and who are
condemned to dance non-stop for a whole year, in agony. This story was a very popular one in the Middle Ages, from William of Malmesbury onwards.

La processioun au maufey.
4   Par jour de feste assemblee
Trestouz suhent la meyn senestre . . .

— the diabolical nature of the dance is stressed by all the influential
preachers and exempla-collections, usually associating it with sexual titil-
lation and the wantonness of women. Jacques de Vitry compares women
who sing and lead the dance either to traps set to ensnare dancers like so
many quails:

. . . Mulier enim cantans in chorea est velut instrumentum dyaboli,
quod gallice dicitur 'quailliers' . . .[4]

— or to belled cows heard by the devil and recognised as his own:

. . . Sicut vacca que alias precedit in collo campanam gerit, sic mulier
que prima cantat coream ducit quasi campanam dyaboli ad collum
habet ligatam. Quando autem dyabolus sonum audit securus redditur
dicens: 'Nondum vaccam meam amisi.'[5]

As for the dance itself, Jacques de Vitry likens the *rondet* to the circle
of Hell: 'Chorea enim circulus est, cujus centrum est diabolus, et omnes
vergunt in sinistrum';[6] this last detail may be compared with Bozon's
meyn senestre — the left-hand direction of the dance leading to Hell, just
as in Last Judgement iconography Hell's mouth gapes open to the left-
hand of Christ or St Michael.[7]

The Dominican Etienne de Bourbon traces dancing eruditely back to
Ancient Egypt, but is in no doubt as to its ultimate origins: 'Diabolus est
choreizancium et danciarum inventor et gubernator et procurator';[8] and
he has a story to tell of a demon capering upon the head of a dancing
woman and shaking it from side to side.[9] Similarly, the *Liber exemplorum*
gives a gruesome account of two young dancers having their limbs and
bodies jerked about by devils, like puppets:

[4] *Sermones vulgares*, edited by Crane, p. 114.
[5] Ibid., p. 131.
[6] Paris BN MS f. lat. 17509, fol. 146[r]; cf. Lecoy de la Marche, *La Chaire française* . . . , p. 447.
[7] In his *Contes moralisés* Bozon returns to this image to tell of two companions:
'. . . Lors dit le sage al fol: "Tenoms ceste veie a destre." "Nenyl," fet l'autre, "mes
sués moy; ci gist la voye a senestre." A ceo s'en alerent e od larouns encountre-
rent, e furent despoilez e batuz e affraiez . . .' (edited by Meyer and Toulmin Smith,
pp. 51–52) — the two paths leading respectively to Good and Evil, and the footpads
being the creatures of the Devil.
[8] A. Lecoy de la Marche, *Anecdotes historiques, légendes et apologues tirés du
recueil inédit d'Etienne de Bourbon, dominicain du XIIIe siècle* (Paris, 1877), p. 397.
[9] Ibid., p. 226.

... Movit demon sessor unius brachium eius, et secundum motum eius pulsavit ille socium suum. Movit sessor alterius coxam illius, et juxta motum eius fecit conatum ad socium suum . . .[10]

— all the revellers are likewise affected, men and women, and are danced off into the pit. The *Speculum laicorum* concentrates on the cautionary example of one dance-loving girl who, after her death, was seen in a vision twisting and turning in the fires of Hell, with the same cavorting to which she had abandoned herself when alive and dancing. . . .[11]

With the *Tabula exemplorum* we are perhaps near the 'escripture' mentioned by Bozon as his nominal source of inspiration; this text describes dancing in precisely similar terms:

... Nota coree sunt processiones diaboli; in quibus diabolus precinit et eas ducit. . . .[12]

Having established the theme of the procession, Bozon now adopts his own interpretation; the spirit of the medieval carnival was in essence 'le monde à l'envers', and this is the particular aspect he chooses to lampoon. He pictures all the happy sinners dancing along — but for all the world like a true religious gathering: the whole event becomes a perverted church service, with priest and clerk, banner and bell to summon the sleepers:

> ... E unt lur clers e lur prestre,
> E unt lur banere e lur cloche
> 8   Ke les dormanz laundreit broche.

— but their church-bell is nothing other than the minstrel's drum:

> La cloche, si est lur tabour
> Ke somount les fous pur fere honour
> A Sathanas, e deshonour
> 12   Au seynt ke deyt le sentyme jour.

The attitude of medieval moralists towards the jongleur is predictably harsh: minstrels are accounted sinners and lewd fellows, society's parasites. The Church forbade the giving of alms to minstrels (who were commonly rewarded in kind), and this stern example was followed notably by the jongleur-hating Philippe-Auguste of France:

... pour ce que li bon rois regarda que toutes ces choses estoient faites pour le boban et pour la vanité dou siecle, si estoit contraire a l'ame et

---

[10] 'De ludis inordinandis', edited by Little, pp. 109–10.
[11] See the edition by Welter, p. 33.
[12] See the edition by Welter, p. 11.

d'autre part il ramenoit a memoire ce que il avoit oï dire a aucuns reli-
gieus, que cil qui done a tiex menesteriex, il fait sacrifice au deable, il
voua et proposa en son cuer que tant com il vivoit il donroit ses viez
robes aus povres genz revestir. . . .[13]

In Bozon's lines the minstrel leading the dance and singing foolish fic-
tions acts as some perverted priest attendant upon a monstrous heresy,
accompanied by acolytes of both sexes clad in dress rather more becoming
than surplices:

<blockquote>

16

Lur prestre est dit cely ou cele
Ke comence chant de sote favele;
Les autres ke suhent, mal e femele,
Apelez sunt les clers de sa chapele.
En lu de sourplus lur sunt baillez
Blaunche cheynses ben ridees.
</blockquote>

— here the puritanical preacher jibes at the worldly luxury of such idle
folk who, not satisfied with sober surplices, compound their crime with
the sin of vanity. A freshly-pressed and laundered costume was accounted
particularly desirable in fashionable medieval circles; witness again Jehan
Renart:

<blockquote>
. . . La dame estoit devant la sale
Qui n'ama onques chainse sale . . .[14]
</blockquote>

and:

<blockquote>
. . . Ja mes, voir, en lieu ou ge soie
Ne verrai gent a tel solaz,
Ne tante dame estroite a laz,
En chainses ridez lor biauz cors. . . .[15]
</blockquote>

For Bozon, however, there is nothing praiseworthy in such garments.
'Vanitas' heads a long list of cautionary complaints in the various exempla-
collections, and the practical misogyny of the Middle Ages is very evident
in the continual attacks on female fashions and make-up. Bozon will return
to a more direct assault upon such fripperies in his sixth sermon; here he
contents himself with an added warning to the 'parishioners' who bring

---

[13] *Les grandes chroniques de France*, edited by J. Viard (Paris, 1930), VI, 155.
The *Manuel des Péchés* (edited by Furnivall, vv. 4355-90) relates a tale drawn from
St Gregory of a *munestral* who disturbs a bishop's Grace at table with his singing, and
who on leaving the building with his pay is struck dead by a falling stone.
[14] *Guillaume de Dole*, edited by Lecoy, vv. 3261-62.
[15] Ibid., vv. 194-97.

up the rear of this unholy procession, and who so wholeheartedly enjoy being led a dance by the minstrel-priest:

Les autres ke ne chantent mye,
20   Mes un[t] delit en lur folie
E les aboutent en my les dens
Sunt apaleez lur paroisiens.
En checun atyffure de teste e de pee
24   Un coutel au deable si est liveré,
Pur oscyr les almes en cele assemblé.

— in each little adornment, from top to toe, there lies hidden a hellish blade, ready to stab the wearer's soul. We may imagine the friar looking fiercely down upon his own congregation of *paroissiens* at this point, as he brings his example home at the end:

Ceo dit le livere en bone verité;
Ly sage prestre ben le freyt
28   Ke ceste chose en sarmon deyt,
E si nul en seyt grevé
De bon quer seyt pardoné.
             AMEN.

The particular conceit employed by Bozon in this sermon, the carnival-dance as mock church service, is a remarkably telling one; it is taken up again, later in the fourteenth century, by the Dominican John de Bromyard in his *Summa predicantium*, in an acid commentary on dancing: in the service of the 'church of the malignants' the flute-player is the clerk, high fashion the altar-piece, and a love-ditty the hymn, with the parishioners more raptly held than ever they were by proper mass or sermon.[16]

It should be noted that the medieval Church was not hostile to all forms of dancing, but did distinguish between the worldly and the decent; where Christ was Lord of the Dance, all was permitted, and the mystical ecstasy of the 'Dance of the Cross' was a feature of Franciscan lyricism. Even so, the preachers' attacks on wanton dancing are among the most severe to be found levelled against any vain occupation. Certainly, contemporary examples, and their aftermaths, were all too available: Etienne de Bourbon describes how a church in the Soissons diocese, which had been profaned by dancing, was destroyed by fire from Heaven, with great loss of life; and he follows this account with the ghastly story of the son of Gui V, Count of Nevers and Forez, who perished with his companions during Christmas revelry at the château of Sury-le-Comtal, when the floor

16 Cf. H. Owst, *Literature and Pulpit* . . . , p. 394.

on which they were dancing gave way (Etienne himself arrived in time to
see the shambles, the very next day).[17]

Given these actual examples of Divine Wrath, it is easy to understand
the sermon warnings of such friars as Nicholas Bozon and the compilers of
the exempla-collections; and even these cautionary tales pale when set
against the extraordinary and shocking case of the Inverkeithing Dancers
of Fife, as reported, s.a. 1282, by an outraged Lanercost Chronicle:

> . . . About this time in Easter week, the parish priest of Inverkeithing,
> named John, revived profane rites of Priapus, collecting young girls
> from villages and compelling them to dance in circles to Father Bacchus.
> When he had these females in a troop, out of sheer wantonness he led
> the dance, carrying in front on a pole a representation of the human
> organs of reproduction; and singing and dancing himself like a mime, he
> viewed them all and stirred them to lust by filthy language . . .[18]

– a *processioun au maufey*, indeed.

[17] See the edition by Lecoy de la Marche, pp. 398–99.
[18] *Chronicon de Lanercost*, edited by J. Stevenson (Glasgow, Maitland Club,
1839), p. 109; translated by H. Maxwell (Glasgow, 1913). John was later stabbed to
death, and not surprisingly.

THE FOURTH SERMON:
MAN'S CONTRARY NATURE

Coment nous sumus si contrarious
a nostre seygnur k'est sy dous.

The monorhymed stanzas of this verse sermon capture very well the preacher's hard insistence, as he dwells unremittingly on his theme. This is the bleakest and most accusing of Bozon's texts, the poet seeking to expose man's contrary and perverse nature, and to point out the terrible risk he runs as a result. The exposition of the opening lines presents the classic *ensample* of medieval moralising: the pressing need to admit, to confess and to repent one's sins if one is to be saved:

	Ky de touz maus quert allegaunce
I	Preygne ensample par meynte cheaunce
	De soun pecché aver peysaunce,
4	E fere (fol. 82ᵛ) amendes par penaunce ...

— here, then, is the friar preaching the essential text of his mission, holding forth on the duty of confession and repentance, and following in the tradition formalised by Lateran IV a century earlier and spread through a host of Latin and vernacular works. The half-practical, half-mystical order of progression is an established one: a contrite spirit, a purging confession, a redeeming act of penance.[1]

Having made this vital initial point, Bozon looks about him rhetorically and observes how little effect all this teaching seems to have had; there is an ominous gap between sin and penance, as sinners think it folly (*tenir a enfance*) to repent their sins, despite the consequences:

	Mes ben say par la destaunce
	Ke est entre pecché e penaunce,
	Ke peccheour tent [a] enfaunce
8	De pecché aver repentaunce;
	E si n'est jour ke ne wyn[e] grewance
	Pur nostre pecché par vengaunce,

---

[1] Thus the *Speculum laicorum*: 'Sunt autem penitencie tres partes: 1° contricio . . . 2° confessio . . . 3° satisfactio, que tres habet partes, sc. jejunium . . . oracio . . . elemosina' (edited by Welter, pp. 88–89); and thus the great thirteenth-century exemplum of *Le Chevalier au Barisel*: '. . . que Diex, qui en la crois fu mis, / vous mece a vrai penitanche / et vous doinst tant de repentanche / ke vous conissiés vos pechiés . . .' (edited by F. Lecoy, Paris, CFMA, 1955, vv. 294–97).

Ne ja pur ceo de mesfesaunce
12   Ne recrehoums pur nule cheaunce.

— all the woes (*grewance*) that daily descend on our heads still fail to move us in the right direction, to retract and to repent of our misdeeds (*mesfesaunce*).

This theme is elaborated in Stanza II, which swiftly adds the question of sincerity to the general issue of repentance. Bozon cuttingly points out that a sinner in distress finds himself the unhappy bedfellow of his past actions, and is quick enough to promise to mend his ways, in the hope of relief (*allegaunce*); but then is equally quick to break his word after little or no amends, and slide back comfortably into folly:

II   En tens de anguse regeysoums
            Male pecché ke fet awoums,
            En souzspiraunt par te somouns
16   De nus amender promittoums,
            Si allegaunce en eums;
            Nostre promés oblyhoums,
            Poy hou nent amendoums,
20   Mes tut a folie acordoums.

— there is here more than a hint of the intolerable contradiction between 'dire' and 'fere' pilloried as hypocrisy by many moral satirists from the early thirteenth century onwards (including, notably, the poet Rutebeuf). Bozon illustrates his point with a telling sequence of antitheses that all speak of a wantonly perverse attitude towards the Lord, and that end the stanza on a note of frustration:

            Si Deu nus manace, force ne fesoums;
            Sy il nous bate, nous deseporoums;
            Si il nous dauncele, fous devenoums;
24   Si yl nous atent, tant plus targoums.

This is the picture that Bozon paints and in which he invites his listeners to recognise themselves: his sinners (among whom he soberly includes his own person) are careless of God's warnings, but in despair when struck down; should they on the other hand enjoy the Lord's favour (the *dauncele* of v. 23 describes a caress, as of a spoilt child, or a lover), they may well be ecstatic, but will still dally, and keep him waiting in the end. The wealth of feeling and depth of irony are very finely conveyed in these few expertly counterpointed lines.

With the third stanza Bozon draws a still firmer contrast between human sin and heedlessness, and God's perfection and compassion. On the one hand the offer of salvation as God waits to see if he is heeded:

III   Mes tant est Deu de homme tendre,
           Tut nous put il par mort susprendre,
           Par sa douzour nous vult attendre
28   Pur ver ky voudra vers ly entendre ...

— but on the other hand the poet sees the whole of human society, high and low, sinning blatantly and striving all the more to outrage the Creator, even as he waits:

           Cum plus atent de nous reprendre,
           E plus afforzoum de ly offendre:
           Ceo pert au secle par mesprendre
32   De povre e riche, meyndre e greyndre.

The preacher's pessimism now redoubles; like many moralists before and after him he sees the ominous triumph of evil, with shame fallen in the dust, sin growing apace and torment begetting torment:

           Hounte faut e chet en cendre,
           Pecché crest, e peyne engendre.
           Si vous plest a mey entendre,
36   La resoun pur quey powez aprendre.

— thus inspired, he now turns upon his congregation, requests their close attention, and embarks on a detailed exposition of his *resoun* in an extended final stanza. From this point allegorical figures rise up to dominate the conclusion of the sermon, and to shift its emphasis from an attack on man's wilfulness to a still more powerful lament on the state of the world. Here Bozon follows the classic didactic tradition of the Psychomachia, derived from the fourth-century Christian poet Prudentius: of an essential and mighty conflict, a dramatic battle between the forces of Good and Evil. Originally this motif presented the inevitable triumph of virtue over vice in a succession of 'single combats'; but Bozon — again in common with many moralists and satirists from the thirteenth century — chooses to show the outcome in radically different terms, as most monstrous and perverted: the vices reign, the virtues beat a retreat in a world given over to evil. This theme of the decline of old values runs through OF literature both homiletic and courtly, and blends tellingly with the lament of the 'ubi sunt' tradition:

           ... Mes li tens est si atornez
           Qu'en ne troeve mes qui bien face ...

— complains Jehan Renart,[2] shaking his head at the fall of social graces; while the poet Aubertin d'Arraines, in a more moralising spirit, goes further still:

> Fois, loiaulteis, solais et cortoixie
> Voi, se m'est vis, en mainte gens fineir;
> Deloiaultés est sovent essaucie,
> Le siecle voi durement triboleir. . . .[3]

It is this idea of the world out of joint that Bozon takes up and makes his own in a sequence of vivid and lamenting parallel antitheses. His chosen virtues and their out-matching vices are: Fidelity and Falseness, Love and Malice, Generosity and Avarice, Pity and Hatred, Chastity and Lust, 'Courtoisie' and Usury, and 'Naturesce' and Covetousness:

IV   Ja Leauté tapit e se cele,
         Fausine se moustre e revele;
         De Amour ne peert ja une estencele,
40   Mes tut est allumee de Malice l'astele;
         Largesce se byngne en petit urcele,
         E Chynchesce se baynne en large paele.
         Pyté en flestryt, Haunge renovele;
44   Lecherye est reyne, Chausteté auncele;
         Courtesie dort, Usure chaele;
         Naturesce est baraynne, Coveityse angnele.

All these allegorical figures, it should be noted, represent human relationships which a popular Franciscan preacher might be expected to stress in his admonishing sermons against egoism and worldliness; and Bozon is highly adept at bringing them to life by means other than by standard ritual personification. He describes them in practical, colloquial terms, and has them perform physical antics. 'Leauté' is seen cowering and hiding in a corner, while the triumphant 'Fausine' struts about openly; *faucine* is an Anglo-Norman term denoting treacherous disloyalty, and is picked out by Bozon in his *Contes moralisés* in a similar preaching attack: '. . . pur vostre faucyne . . . vous serrez en enferne perdurablement . . .'[4] 'Amour''s light has flickered out, leaving everything to be lit by the kindling of 'Malice'. While 'Largesce' (that most noble of social and moral medieval virtues) is forced to slink away to crouch in a little jug, mean 'Chynchesce' wallows

[2] *Guillaume de Dole*, edited by Lecoy, vv. 553–54.
[3] *Chansons satiriques et bachiques*, edited by A. Jeanroy and A. Langfors (Paris, CFMA, 1921), p. 5 (vv. 1–4).
[4] 'Quod amor mundanus post mortem cito evanescit'; see the edition by Meyer and Toulmin Smith, p. 103.

at ease in a large pan. It is typical of Bozon that he should enliven his
serious sermon with such earthy imagery, drawn from popular vocabulary.
These particular items of kitchen-ware are used in sayings by way of striking contrast, to express a descent into neglect or hard times: the smallness
of the *urcele/orcel* being set against the large size of another utensil, be it
pan, pot or tub.[5]

The miser's damnation is a standard theme of medieval moralising; and
Bozon's horror at the earthly triumph of avarice is certainly shared by the
Franciscan exempla-compilers. The *Liber exemplorum* breaks into English,
quoting a suitable doggerel-couplet to conclude its various attacks:

> Hym were bettre that he ne were ne never boren,
> For liif and soule he his forloren . . .[6]

— while the *Tabula exemplorum* likens a dead miser to the carcase of an
ass thrown to a pack of dogs:

> . . . cum moritur pellis temporalium extrahitur, corpus vermibus datur
> et anima canibus infernalibus . . .[7]

— and the *Speculum laicorum* insultingly compares the miser to glutin-
ous mire, and to a pig that is only good when slaughtered.[8]

Bozon's sad list continues, with 'Pyté' withering and 'Haunge' blooming
like some unnatural flower; 'Lecherye' is queen, while 'Chausteté' so be-
loved of the Franciscans is a Cinderella serving-maid. 'Courtesie' slumbers,
and allows 'Usure' to rule the roost; this is *cortoisie* in its sense of 'fairness',
'proper behaviour': a great social and moral virtue linked to the ever-
desirable *mesure*, and as here the very opposite of the unfairness of usury.
In his *Contes moralisés* Bozon makes Usury one of the Devil's hunting-
dogs, answering to the pet name of 'Treble-up':

> . . . Un autre chien ad descouplee qe est Trebelyn apellé, ceo est a dire
> usure, as marchauntz, par quoy pechent plusours e cheient en laz au
> deable. E pur ceo est apellé Trebelyn ceo chien qe lur chace, qar rien ne
> vendrount ne apresterount ne achateront si ils ne eyent le treble a
> gayn . . .[9]

— and here too Bozon laments the fact that *le siecle est ore bestornee*,
and that as a result usurers are no longer scorned but are honoured even by

[5] Tobler-Lommatzsch, *Altfranzösisches Wörterbuch*, VI, 1186: 'Proecce, vus
dormés et malvestés oisiele;/ Hui cest jor estes mise de le cuve en ouciele. . . .'
[6] See the edition by Little, p. 45.
[7] See the edition by Welter, p. 5.
[8] See the edition by Welter, p. 14.
[9] See the edition by Meyer and Toulmin Smith, p. 35.

the highest lords in the land. His fellow-moralisers express similar revulsion: exemplary stories abound, telling of a usurer having his mouth filled with red-hot coins,[10] or being dragged on board the Devil's ship, or being devoured by serpents.[11] With their clear insistence on the virtue of poverty, the Franciscans were above all intent on condemning what they saw as a growing evil, in an increasingly trade-conscious medieval society; the *Speculum laicorum*, always methodical in its approach, identifies six types of usury and codifies again into six the various effects of the vice.[12]

'Naturesce' is depicted as a barren woman looking on while the all-too-fertile 'Coveityse' whelps; Bozon employs the term *naturesce* to define a nobility of human spirit, akin to fidelity.[13] In Continental French, Guillaume le Clerc draws a similar opposition between Covetousness and *franchise*:

> . . . Quant Damnedeus sema franchise,
> E li dïables coveitise. . . .[14]

Bozon brings his psychomachia towards its end; his final scene is the truly hellish one of a world possessed by the spirits of evil:

	Ire e Felonye echaufent la bouhele,
48	Losenge e Mensonge tournent la rouhele;
	Male Fame court, la Bone si chauncele,
	E ordure fleyre cum mire [ou] kanele.
	Mes brevement a dire de checune parcele:
52	Le mound ne fest autre fors alme flaele!

In order to illustrate to the utmost the effect produced upon the hapless world by the most violent and warped allegorical personalities of Wrath and Felony, Trickery and Untruth, Bozon chooses with skill a grisly double-layered image. The OF colloquial expression *echauffer la boele* means 'to enrage (s.o.)', 'to stir up fury', and as such is used very aptly here to describe the deeds of 'Ire e Felonye'. Similarly, there is a common medieval saying *Mal torne la roele*, 'Ill-met!', 'Woe-the-day!'; the picture is that of the Wheel of Fortune, and here depicts — again appropriately — a society turned topsy-turvy, with 'Losenge e Mensonge' tugging the wheel down.

[10] Jacques de Vitry, *Sermones vulgares*, edited by Crane, p. 72.

[11] Etienne de Bourbon, edited by Lecoy de la Marche, pp. 367–69.

[12] See the edition by Welter, pp. 110–11.

[13] Compare *Contes moralisés* ch. 81, describing an eagle symbolic of goodness: 'Querez donqe cel oysel qe vole ci haut par amour de longe duree, par deus eles qe le portent: leauté e naturesce . . .' (see the edition by Meyer and Toulmin Smith, p. 101). The opposite quality, 'Denaturesce', is also used by Bozon in his *Contes* and in his specific *tretis*, with the prime meaning of the unnatural greed of ingrate sons.

[14] *Le Besant Dieu*, edited by P. Ruelle (Brussels, 1973), vv. 1715–16.

Once put together in a couplet, however, these two images may take on an added and even more sinister connotation, that of medieval torture; the four Vices become masked executioners, disembowelling their victims and breaking them on the wheel. A comparable example of this torture-chamber usage is found in the Chanson de geste *Foulques de Candie*:

> ... Et ces deus que ci voi metrai en tele roele
> Que li uns traira l'autre lo cuer ou la boele. ...[15]

The growth of *losenge* in medieval society is an ill lamented and condemned in a host of courtly and moralising texts from the beginning of the thirteenth century. The figure of the *losengier*, the cunning Iago-like trickster who delights in the publication and destruction of secret love-affairs, enters Romance literature in both male and female form, and adopts the standard role of menacing false-flatterer. Bozon will twice attack the *losengeour* in his *Contes moralisés*: once aptly retelling Aesop's fable of the Fox and the Cheese to illustrate the chapter 'Quod verba adulatoria minuunt vitia et virtutes'; and again as a gloss to Ecclesiasticus 5. 14 ('Be not called a whisperer, and lie not in wait with thy tongue: for a foul shame is upon the thief, and an evil condemnation upon the double tongue'):

> ... Par double lange est homme esprovee ... un de medisauntz e un autre de losengeaunce ...[16]

— it is thus hardly surprising that 'Losenge' is singled out for attack in his sermon.

Bozon follows up the shocking image of torture with a brutal 'jeu du bestourné': the illustration of black made white by the triumph of evil; with Good Repute tottering like an invalid and Ill-Fame sprinting ahead, nothing is any longer as it should be, and 'shit smells as sweetly as myrrh or cinnamon' (v. 50). Bozon never declines a coarse phrase if it will serve his purpose and strengthen his sermon; this particular one obviously appeals to him in its very grotesqueness, since he employs it again in expanded form in one of the *Contes moralisés* to describe a character's foul breath.[17]

At this striking point the catalogue of sin and woe ceases, and the

---

[15] vv. 11, 234; compare Tobler-Lommatzsch, *Altfranzösisches Wörterbuch*, VIII, 1376–77.

[16] See the edition by Meyer and Toulmin Smith, pp. 14–15, 159.

[17] No. 23 (see the edition by Meyer and Toulmin Smith, pp. 37–38). This is a version of the animal fable of the lion who could tolerate neither truth nor flattery from his minions (cf. La Fontaine's *La cour du lion*); after the goat has been killed for having said of the lion's reeking breath: 'Il puit vilement', the colt meets a similar fate for stating the opposite: 'Sire ... vostre aleyne plus douce odure que mirre ou canele.'

preacher suddenly concludes his poem on a note of ultimate warning, that the evil world he has depicted will prove a scourge to the soul. So ends the fourth sermon, abruptly and without any concluding 'Amen'. It may be noted that the scribe has also omitted his customary concluding-bracket after v. 52; but this should not automatically imply an incomplete ending. As it stands the construction of Stanza IV, with its extra quatrain acting almost as an envoi, rounds the poem off quite satisfactorily; and in any case Bozon himself indicates an abrupt and thought-provoking conclusion with his conventional *brevement a dire* in v. 51. His images throughout the text have served as hammer-blows in their brutality and realism; here he threatens fire and sulphur, and with no anticlimactic terminal prayer an 'Amen' would appear inappropriate. He is intent on stressing his homiletic point that man's wanton blindness has led to vice triumphant, and that present pleasure leads to future pain. His next sermon follows on both literally (on the next line of manuscript) and logically, dealing indeed with the practical question raised by the previous text: how man may make best use of his time on earth.

THE FIFTH SERMON:
HARVEST OF LIFE

Coumparisoun al haust de ceste vie.

This text sets out a very straightforward basic simile freshened by the poet's individual style; in an orthodox symbolism of the seasons, life is likened to 'August', the harvest season. This Bozon expands in the opening lines into an exemplum drawn from the world of farming and husbandry. He describes how a man will labour long in the hot weather in order to garner food and sustenance; not daring to lose one single day during this brief summer season, he willingly suffers now for future gain, and considers his sweat and arduous labour small price to pay for a bumper harvest:

	Ceste vie resemble al haust,
	Kant povres homme ne let pur chaud
	De travailler forciblement,
4	Pur soustenaunce ke au cors apent;
	En cele sesoun porte fés,
	Pur estre meuz [a]hese aprés.
	Mout harreyt un bon overour
8	Perdre en haust un bon jour:
	Sun travail prent a leger
	Kant entent le bon lower.
	En cele sesoun ke poy dure,
12	Se quert viaunde e vesture
	E se fet a malhese
	De estre aprés meuz a hese.
	De lu en lu se quert overaynne,
16	Ke par (fol. 83ʳ) travail le plus gaynne;
	E pur le gayn ke veyt devaunt ly
	Tout soun travail met en obly.

— the vocabulary here is a deliberate listing and restressing of two key and counterpointing elements: of burden (*travailler forciblement, fés, overaynne, travail, malhese*) and recompense (*soustenaunce, hese, lower, gayn*). Of all these motifs, that of *lower* ('reward') is perhaps the most essential; and Bozon will return in some detail to it in this sermon, and subsequently.

The poet has pointed out how essential it is for a poor man to labour in

this fashion: a poor man quite simply cannot afford to miss the opportu-
nity. It would thus be terrible if he were to be struck down at this crucial
time by illness, and be unable to reap his harvest:

> Ke dirra dounke ly mendifs
> 20   Ke tant cum chaumpe de frut est plentifs
> Destourbé est par maladie
> De travailler e quere aÿe?

Bozon is dealing here in simple practicalities; he goes on to paint a vivid
and realistic picture of the privations suffered by just such an unfortunate
at Christmastide, when all other folk are in party mood and costume; he is
a prey to hunger and cold because through his illness he has not the where-
withal to clothe and feed himself:

> Pleyndre se pourra au nouhel,
> 24   Kant autres serrunt vestuz bel,
> E de famyne e de freyt,
> Pur ceo ke malade avant esteit
> Kant ke devereyt purchacer
> 28   Vivere e vesture par travailler.
> Lors purra chanter, 'Allas! allas!'
> Kant autrez serrount en lur solaz.

— as always, Bozon manages to find images that are instantly recognisable by his congregation: those same listeners that include the young
wastrels condemned in the first sermon and the gourmands arraigned in
the second sermon's allegory on table etiquette. They certainly would
appreciate the extent of the disaster that would befall a man no longer
able to afford worldly pleasures and parties. The whole of the exposition
has stressed material considerations, and the preacher now moves forward
to the glossing of his parable, and to turn his listeners' minds dramatically
to more spiritual matters. The harvest month clearly enough represents
Man's brief life, during which space it is up to him to labour and deserve
the future heavenly recompense:

> Hore escotez, ke jeo vus die
> 32   Ke cest ensaumple sygnefie:
> La courte vie ke homme vist
> E[st] nostre haust de grant profit,
> Par ky nous pohum en poy de houre
> 36   Louher quere ke touz jours dure,
> Par penaunce e par aumoynne,
> E par merite de vie bone.

Bone vie est prouesce,
40   E male vie est feblesce.
Ke doute homme sun pouher
A deservir bon louher?

One recognises the cardinal feature of the friar's sermonising, the mendicant's stress on present hardship set against eternal reward, on the importance of penitent acts of charity and on the essential merit in *bone vie*, the very strength of which contrasts with the weakness of a wasted life; man should not doubt his ability to gain the true recompense.

The next stage is the unfolding of the allegory of the hapless ill man, who is now seen as one confined to the bed of sin:

Dont cyl est malade en ceste vie
44   Ke n'ad cure de bone vie,
Mes de pecché tent le lyt
Cum cyl ke en haust malade gist,
E pert le temps de purchacer
48   E par tant le tens de louher ...

— thus he loses his chance of spiritual saving. At this point Bozon injects into his sermon a necessary element of accusation, a further attack on human perverseness:

E nekedent teu maladie
Plet a plusurs de ceste vie,
Pur une cheytif bref solaz:
52   N'est autre chose for wereglaz
Ke fet la gent werglacer,
E les almes enpaluer.

The poet has seized upon the irony of this situation, of sinners actually enjoying their deadly malady, and now offers a final striking antithetical image, running parallel with the original parable of winter cold overtaking summer heat: the deceiving warmth of this *bref solaz* is in fact but treacherous ice, *wereglaz* that causes men to slip and fall, and their souls to be covered in filth.[1] With this in mind, Bozon addresses his listeners one final time, and beseeches them to consider the brief space

[1] Compare the *Vers de la Mort* (edited by Wulff and Walberg, V. 1-3): 'Morz, qui nos a toz pris al laz / Qui en toz lieus fais verreglaz / Por nos faire verreglacier. ...' Bozon may have borrowed this image from Hélinant, changing the subject from death to sinful life; his choice of *enpaluer* (to befoul) may equally have been influenced by an earlier line in the *Vers de la Mort* (III. 9-10): 'Qui quiers les voies et les sentes / O l'en se seut empaluer. ...'

allotted to them on earth; if they wish to behave well, then they must dili-
gently seek out all the ways of gaining merit:

	Pur ceo, seygnurs, enpensez
56	Ke poy de temps ycy avez;
	Si vous seyez de bone parz,
	Vous troverez ben de tute parz
	En mout de maneres pur meryr
60	Grant louher au departyr.

— for a fifth time he repeats his telling motif of heavenly reward; and
he ends his sermon most appropriately with another image drawn from the
farm, illustrating the fact that one must wait a time before harvesting the
fruit of one's labours:

	Hore est temps a despendre:
	Aprés ert tens a reprendre.
	Nule ne put huy semer
64	E meme le jour le blé syer;
	Attendre covent la sesoun
	De chescune chose, ceo est resoun.
	Ceo ke ycy deservyrez
68	En le autre vye le troverez:
	Deu nus doynt issy merir
	Ke nous pussum a ly venyr.

AMEN

This is the great Franciscan message: all things have their season, and
one must labour now to profit later; everyone shall have his just deserts in
the life to come.

Bozon's particular skill in sermonising is well in evidence in this short
and uncomplicated poem. He presents a smooth and easily-digested *ensaumple*, moves into the moralising interpretation carefully without losing
the attention of his listeners, touches a sudden note of cold menace, and
brings all with him in his homiletic conclusion and exhortation, ending as
he began with a scene of husbandry. The basic moral image sustained in his
sermon stems ultimately from the scriptural theme 'Whatsoever a man
soweth, that shall he also reap' (Galatians 6. 7), and also from the parallel
warning (Ecclesiastes 3. 1) that 'To every thing there is a season.' The
medieval taste for such examples of Divine harmony and ordered rhythm
is clearly shown in the very common iconography of the Labours of the
Month in illuminations, carving and stained glass, where August is almost
invariably represented by a hard-working harvester, and December often

depicts the direct contrast of merriment and relaxation. 'Labor' is a self-evident virtue, and manual effort in the open air was particularly favoured by the Franciscans who were ever ready to approve the honest toil of simple people.[2] Thus the *Fasciculus Morum* mentions ploughing, sowing and reaping as 'bonae occupationes';[3] and the *Tabula exemplorum* contrasts a field made fertile by dint of hard weeding with one weedless but also unproductive.[4] The implication is that the very harshness of the labour contributes to the ultimate profit; this Bozon states clearly both in his sermon and in his *Contes moralisés*:

> . . . Qar nul rien en ceste vie tant vaut pur cors e alme qe travaille bien
> ordenee. . . . Travail est la vie de homme e gardeyn de sauntee; travaille
> enchace enchesoun de pecheer et fet homme sei mesmes reposer, de
> langur est allegeaunce, a maladie resteaunce, savacioun des gentz,
> acueson de touz les senz, marastre a peresce e norice de leesce, deitee
> as joenes gentz, e merite as veillis genz. . . .[5]

The idea of Man as a potentially bad harvester of the August of his life is found as salutary illustration in other moralising poems, notably in Guillaume le Clerc's *Besant Dieu* (c. 1226–27):

> L'aüst senefie cel jor . . .
> Fols crestïens, dolenz chaitis,
> Levez vos eulz, dresciez vos vis,
> Esgardez com aoust est pres,
> Qui ne retornera jamés!
> Ja sont prest e meuür li blé:
> Que cueldreiz vus? q'ai'vos semé?[6]

— and the parable duly continues with the figure of the idle man neglecting his spiritual crops. What sets Bozon's little sermon apart is the poet's inventive touch that enables him to weave into his homily a handful of scenes of great realism: the wretched threadbare farmer moaning at the sight of the Christmas revels from which he is barred, and the sinner slipping on the ice and falling in the mire.

It is only appropriate that the allegory of the improvident farmer should

[2] This enthusiasm was naturally not confined to the mendicant orders: two of Jacques de Vitry's sermons are addressed specifically to Husbandmen and Labourers (see the edition by Crane, p. xlv).

[3] Compare Little, p. 156.

[4] See the edition by Welter, p. 41: 'Item ager plus amatur qui post spinas et tribulos uberes fructus attulit quam ille qui numquam spinas habuit et tamen semper sterilis est . . .'.

[5] See the edition by Meyer and Toulmin-Smith, p. 142.

[6] See the edition by Ruelle, vv. 1647, 2839–44.

find a highly practical echo in the strictures of an actual Anglo-Norman treatise on Husbandry, that of Walter de Henley:

> . . . Wos veet une gens ke unt teres e tenemens e i ne sevent pas vivre. Pur quey? jo le wos dirray, pur çoe ke eus vivent santz ordinance fere e purveyance avant mayn, e despendent e gastent plus ke lur teres valent par an, e kant il unt degastés lur bens adonc ne unt fors ke de mayn en gule, e vivent en angoysse . . .[7]

— the estate manager and the preacher have evidently much in common, the one with his distaste for farming wastrels living from hand to mouth, the other with an equal horror of spiritual idlers who neither sow nor reap Heaven's *louher*. Bozon will return to the farm in his eighth sermon, with similar imagery and effects.

[7] *Hosebondrie*, edited by E. Lamond (London, 1890), pp. 2–4.

THE SIXTH SERMON:
ON FOOLISH CHATTER

Une courte ditee
de longe folie usee.

With this 'short ditty on a long-lasting folly' Bozon returns to a justi-
fiably wrathful scrutiny of his individual parishioners. Armed with the
same vigour that has characterised his assaults on dancing and sermon-
ducking, he takes up the subject of 'Jaunglerye', gossiping, and considers
this lamentable failing in the context of an unruly congregation. The church
in medieval society was a great meeting-place and business centre as well as
the Domus Dei: indeed certain parish churches served as covered markets,
with stalls set up along the nave. It is hardly surprising that preachers
should have to contend with a positive tumult of chatter, or that much sermon material that has come down to us should level attacks on the shocking standard of decorum. Bozon's obvious personal feelings here must have
been shared by preachers the length of Western Christendom, and impatience
with this social vice spreads noticeably into medieval literature generally,
with the motif of the *radot*, the nattering dotage that reduces old men to
childishness. Jacques de Vitry tells the story (subsequently to become very
popular) of the devil observed in church on a great holy-day writing down
on a length of parchment all the idle words spoken by the congregation,
and having to stretch it with his teeth to fit them all on.[1] For the *Tabula
exemplorum*, a good congregation is like a hive of attentive bees; but a bad
one, gossiping, joking and arguing, more resembles worthless wasps:

> . . . quidam sunt sicut vespes et burdones, qui mel ab apibus confectum
> devorant. Hii sunt qui aliis orantibus et sacerdote conficiente garriunt
> vel trufant vel quod deterius est, detrahunt vel litigant. . . .[2]

The charge of gossiping is above all made out against women; and here
the preachers reveal all the notorious antifeminism of the Middle Ages.
Women's chatter is like the yapping of low-bred dogs, according to the
Speculum laicorum;[3] and Jacques de Vitry weighs in with an example of
a nun whose chastity was not matched by any reticence of speech: she was
accordingly carried off by demons and burned, from the waist up (the

---

[1] *Sermones vulgares*, edited by Crane, p. 100.
[2] See the edition by Welter, p. 56.
[3] See the edition by Welter, p. 33.

moral being, 'Tolle humilitatem, castitas non placet').[4] The dubious prize must perhaps go to Etienne de Bourbon, for perfecting the stereotype joke of the nagging wife. He tells of a married couple at sea during a storm; at the tempest's height, orders are given to throw all heavy ballast overboard; whereupon:

> . . . ille exhibuit uxorem, dicens quod in tota navi non esset gravius aliquid lingua eius.[5]

— such cautionary tales go hand in hand with the still cruder and more violent antifeminist attacks of the OF fabliaux; and the cruelly practical end is wife-beating and the scold's bridle.

Nicholas Bozon's own broadside against 'jaunglerye' in church is particularly effective for taking the form of a little 'Etats du monde' in close focus. In his congregation are all the estates, of high and low degree, joined alike not in prayer but in raucous gabbling:

> Escotez, seygnours, escotez
> Les folyes ke sunt usez
> De plusurs ke wount a mouster,
> 4   Ke ren ne fount for jaungeler.
> La parlent de vanité
> Chescun soloum sun degré . . .

— the images in the succession of little vignettes that follow are razor-sharp; from the pulpit of Bozon's verse we first look down upon the gentry as they talk on about hunting matters:

> Les gentiz e les fraunks
> 8   Parlent de chens corauns,
> Hou de faucouns ben volaunz.

— throughout the poem Bozon makes use of monorhyme groupings to suit his categorising, and to give his verses the neatly-parcelled effect of epithets. In this case three lines are linked, giving an uneven number to the poem as a whole; it is possible that a line has been lost at this point in the text, but the sense is in no way broken and it is logical to accept the three as complete.

Next is a scene of sheer materialism: the local lord is busy hearing cases brought to his court, while the local officials are coolly carrying out their business, the bailiff taking down sworn statements and the provost collecting the amercements, the fines or levies:

---

[4] See the edition by Crane, pp. 113–14.
[5] See the edition by Lecoy de la Marche, p. 202 ('Sic mulier linguata homini quieto gravissima est ad sustinendum').

> La teent seygnur sez parlemens,
> La prent baillif les seremens,
> 12   La prevost receyt les mercymens:
> Si ne fount a Deu nule reverence.

One should note here that such calculating officers receive very short shrift generally from the Franciscan exempla-compilers who, sharing a distaste obviously felt by the common folk, recount many tales of false or extortionate stewards and bailiffs. The *Speculum laicorum* tells of a particularly abusive and bullying English steward who was doomed after his death to a Sisyphan punishment of cutting off his tongue with a razor and of swallowing the pieces, which then re-formed only to be sliced away anew.[6] Nicholas Bozon shows himself throughout his *Contes moralisés* to be a strong radical in condemning the oppression of the poor by the rich lords of the land and by their servants; the latter he likens to ravening wild boars, and he coldly quotes an English political couplet: 'For ȝif þe louerd bidd sle, þe stiward biddes fle' ('A lord can condemn you to death, but a steward will flay you alive').[7]

Bozon's church has been turned into the local assizes, and this mercenary attitude spills over to affect people who should know better, the various chaplains all intent on finding moneyed patrons who will pay them for praying regularly for their souls in a chantry chapel. And the indiscipline has spread to all ages, to the mocking *juvenceus* who seem positively to plague Bozon, and to their elders (but hardly betters) mulling too audibly over old times:

> La pleyde chapelayn pur dymerie,
> La counte veyllard de auncienerye,
> 16   La fount ly juvenceus lur mokerie, (fol. 83ᵛ)
> La tenent fous lur tenzerye.

— there are even quarrels and disputes breaking out in the house of God!

The rest of the sermon is given over entirely to an attack on the behaviour of the women of the congregation; they are for Bozon prime targets, and he takes delight in pillorying them as they spend their time preening themselves and tattling about expensive clothes and fine saddles, fashion jewellery and hairstyles, new sport and other frivolous trifles:

> La parlent dames e dammeseles
> De riche dras e bele seles,

---

[6] See the edition by Welter, p. 18.
[7] See the edition by Meyer and Toulmin Smith, p. 12.

20   De beau treszours, de corouneles,
                            De noveu geu, de vei ceneles.[8]

Medieval preachers and moralists are even quicker to condemn the vain
finery of women's clothes than they do the vice of female chatter (Bozon
here very neatly combines the two failings). Jacques de Vitry transforms
a typical Pastourelle about a beautiful girl ('Main se leva la bienfaite Aelis
/ Bel se para et plus bel se vesti . . .') into an antifeminist caution against
blatant public vanity:

> . . . Hujusmodi autem mulieres quando ad publicum exire vel etiam ire
> debent, magnam diei partem in apparatu suo consumunt. Quant Aaliz
> fu levee, et quant ele fu lavee, et la messe fu chantee, et deable l'en ont
> emportee . . .[9]

— and elsewhere he compares vain women to peacocks (lovely feathers,
harsh voices), and describes an incident of the devil riding into church
aboard a woman's long train.[10] Etienne de Bourbon similarly abhors fancy
dresses and trains, together with elaborate belts, exaggerated wimples, long-
pointed shoes (too easily seized by the devil), wigs and rouge.[11] John de
Bromyard's *Summa Predicantium* calls over-dressed women 'the devil's
nets', and thunderingly contrasts women's skin-deep beauty with skulls
and rotting flesh.[12] Nicholas Bozon's touch in his sermon is lighter, but no
less effective; he shows his female audience too busy looking round, and
being looked at, to pay the slightest attention to the service. He ruefully
observes that no truly pious girl will dare go to church to say her prayers,
for fear of being jeered at by her unruly sisters; her place is occupied by an
Eve with a new head-dress to show off:

                            Chescun[e] autre tant avise
                            Ke poy attendent au servise;
24   E cele ke vosit volenteres
                            Ses preeres dyre a mousters
                            Pur les autres ne hose pas,
                            Ke de ly freyent lur gas.

---

[8] The MS presents difficult readings, vv. 20–21. *Cenele* (*bot.* 'haw') is found in
OF and Anglo-Norman as an object of minimal worth; *vai* means 'flighty, frivolous';
corouneles would seem to denote a form of head adornment, but this particular
diminutive of *corone* is not found in OF: one would have expected *coro(u)nete*. However, the changing of diminutive endings is not infrequent in Anglo-Norman.

[9] *Sermones vulgares*, edited by Crane, p. 114.

[10] Ibid., pp. 101, 114. Bozon too mocks fashionable trains in his little poem comparing women to magpies.

[11] See the edition by Lecoy de la Marche, pp. 228–42.

[12] Owst, *Literature and Pulpit* . . . , pp. 395–96.

28 Mes la vendra dounkes en place
  Quele dame out plus de grace
  De estre prisee a la feste
  Pur l'atyre de sa teste!

— but there are other matrons in the audience who are equally inattentive but rather less fortunate; Bozon ends his sermon on a note of humorous, if sarcastic, observation by conjuring up three vivid characters, Jill and Joan and their neighbour, all lamenting household disasters — the loss of hens and chickens, the crop of flax ravaged by the birds:

32 E la se pleynt la matrone
  A ses veysynes Gylle e Jone,
  Ke ele ad perdu ces pocyns
  Par felonie de ses veysyns.
36 L'autre respont: 'E par veysynes
  Ay jeo perdu mes gelynes!'
  La terce dit ke tut sun lyn
  Si est destrut par oselyn.

— at which raucous point Bozon swiftly brings his sermon to an end, and urges his listeners to desist from such idle matters:

  Ke sages est [e pros],
  Il lerra teus ocios,
  Et dirra ses preeres de bon quer
  Taunt cum est a mouster.

Bozon's mastery of small-scale observation is very well illustrated in this little piece; and from it one may appreciate the manner in which the friars transformed the art of the sermon into a popular exercise, by preaching without pedantry or scholasticism in a simple and direct fashion. Certainly, no medieval audience of gossips could fail to recognise themselves as portrayed in Bozon's lines, even if they would not always take to heart his final tart injunction.

The Franciscan preacher in Nicholas Bozon was evidently particularly stung by the irritating vice of gossiping. In his satirical *Char d'Orgueil* he rounds (again) on bad chaplains who converse loudly and sing dirty songs:

  ... L'un si chaunte vylenye pur fere les quers soyllez,
  L'autre jaungle en l'eglise, qe autres seyent desturbez ...[13]

— and he deals three passing blows at 'Jaunglerye' in his *Contes moralisés*. In No. 94 we read:

[13] See the edition by Vising, vv. 478-79.

. . . Clerke est honuree pur sa clergie, chivaler pur sa chivalerie, les sotils
pur lur sotilté; mes quant sen est tourné en folie e sotilté en gylerie e
clergie en janglerie, dount l'em fet graund deshonur chescun a cel estat
dount ad receu soun honur . . .[14]

— and again, in No. 116, in a list of birds barred from the Tree of Life:

. . . le egle, pur sa hautenerye, le corf pur sa robberie, le esturnel pur
janglerie, ly perdyz pur lecherie, ly messoun pur sa combaterye, ly
woutre pur sa crueleté. . . .[15]

Finally, Conte no. 71 is completely given over to an attack on wagging
tongues; and it is interesting to compare and contrast Bozon's two sustained criticisms, one in a vigorous finger-jabbing sermon, the other in a
little Elephant-and-Mouse bestiary-fable:

Quod parvipendenda sunt verba stultorum a sapientibus et discretis.

Al oliphant Dieuz ad doné tiel nature qe, tot seit il de tant force q'il
peot porter plusurs gentz bien armez, e de taunt baudour q'il ose assem-
bler a tot un host, uncore il doute un sorice e eschive sa compainie, mes
q'il peut la sorice del un pié quassaer. Et pur qoi le ad Dieux doné tiel
nature, mes pur aprendre les sages, tot seient ils de grand poer, de
ouster les fouz jangelours e eschure lur compaignie? Qar tieuz sount
semblable al sorice qi tolt meynt homme soun repos. . . .[16]

[14] See the edition by Meyer and Toulmin Smith, p. 115.
[15] Ibid., p. 133.   [16] Ibid., p. 91.

THE SEVENTH SERMON:
THE USELESS WILL

Coment les fole genz
se affient trop en testamenz

The weapon of sarcasm which Bozon uses against his unruly, chattering congregation is again deployed, more sharply still, in the following sermon. Nowhere is better illustrated the friar's ability to startle people with near-brutal personal allusions and images, and then to move into the serious meat of his homily. The practical item he seizes on now is a literal 'Item': the last will and testament. The preacher's aim is to shake people into a realisation that it is not enough, for the soul's sake, to make generous bequests after one's death. This is *haut folye*, but one all too common in the *secle*, and one that ensnares too many individuals. Bozon invites us to witness the discomfiture of the dead man who has been reluctant to show any generosity in life, yet who has hoped to redeem all through ample legacies (*testamenz*); we observe the insouciant behaviour of the surviving relatives, who are more ready to sing popular love-ditties after the burial than any Mass of remembrance for the departed's soul:

	Hore escotez, e vous dirrai
	Une haut folye ke trové ay;
	Si est au secle trop usé,
4	D[u]nt meynt homme est engyné
	Ke poynt ne wulent en lur vye
	De lur bens fere courtesie,
	Mes tut se affient en testamenz
8	En heide e socour de lur parenz,
	Ke pur les almes chaunterount
	'Amourettes jolifs me fount!'
	Ceo est la messe ke il averount
12	Aprés le jour ke enterré sunt.

The family is full of joy and rejoicing, with not a thought for the dead man's salvation. They have what they want: the cash. . . . With this telling image Bozon shows how a man that cared for none in his lifetime may expect no care after his death. The scene continues, with its striking likeness to Dickens's *A Christmas Carol*, as the medieval Scrooge — a certain John, or a certain Ralph — is forced to hear some harsh home-truths from the lips of his relations and executors, who cynically neglect the dead to concentrate on the living; there is no need to pray for him if he is in heaven, and no use praying for him if he is elsewhere:

Lors entendrunt lur parlemenz
Executours e parenz:
'Lessez', funt il, 'mort au mort,
16   E vifs de vifs heyent confort!
Cil ke est mort, Johan hou Rauf —
Hou yl est dampné, hou il est sauf;
Si yl est dampné, ne vaut ren
Ke l'em face pur ly de ben!'

— these mercenary kinsmen are all intent on material gain: far from looking back at the dead, they are preoccupied with their future self-interest, with the profitable marriages to be made by their fair and passive children (suitably backed by the recent legacies). Thus Bozon makes his point with apt irony; such examples of post-mortem generosity serve only to cut the bonds between the quick and the dead, and destroy true affection:

'Mes pensum', funt il, 'de nos enfaunz
Ke sunt beaus e taysaunz,
Ke avauncé seyent par mariage:
24   Si froum honour au lignage.'
Assez est sovent esprové
Ke ceste chose est verité:
Les bens ke lessent aprés lur jours
28   Coupent la corde de lel amours
Entre le mors e les vifs,
E de amys funt enemys.

— a very similar cautionary tale is found in the *Contes moralisés*, where Bozon tells of an old fool who bequeaths all his hoarded wealth to his young wife: *si la pria pur Dieu qe ele pensast de lui eyder aprés sa mort*. Unfortunately, she soon remarries, and her new husband, a callous, pleasure-loving minstrel, refuses to spend one penny on a chaplain to pray for the dead man's soul:

'Jeo say . . . meuz chaunter qe le chapeleyn. Emplés deus hanapez, si irroms caroler. Le vaillard fui plus gelous de autres qe de sey, et jeo, qe sui estrange, quai frai jeo pur lui?' Fols est qe se affie en autres aprés sa vie e lest sa alme nuwe pur mettre en estrange muwe. Ceo est a dire en engleys: 'He þat hadd inou to help him self wital, Sithen he ne wold, I ne wile ne I ne schal'. E pur ceo jeo lou qe chescun se enforce de bien fere en sa vie . . .[1]

– the *Speculum laicorum* likewise warns rich sinners against depending too much on executors, quoting an example of a usurer seeking to repent by dividing his ill-gotten wealth among the poor, but being thwarted at his death by his executors who quickly shared out the money between themselves.[2]

The midway moral of Bozon's sermon now appears clear: one must cultivate true friendship during one's lifetime, so that friends whose service will still be needed may continue to honour one after death; and the only way to attract a true friend is by *bone vie*:

	Lors est sage ke s'alye
32	A tele amy en sa vye
	Ke aprés la mort le put trover
	Devaunt ly a grant mester.
	Ky tel amy vout trover
36	Par bone vie le deit aver;
	Deu plus eyme bone vie
	Ke nul tresour de tresorie.

– here Bozon moves with swift logic from attack to homily. What, he asks us, is a 'good life'? He provides the answer with a touching degree of true Franciscan personal humility, citing his study of others and not his personal example:

	Ke est bone vye? vous dirrai
40	Par aprise, n[e]nt par assay.

There now follows the Friar's orthodox exposition of the qualities that go to make up a fitting life; all the items mentioned are found in Franciscan writings generally, and indeed in other works by Bozon. They fall into two main categories: discipline before the Faith, and abasement of Self. The truly good person should love both God and man, and eschew sin. He should attend Mass regularly and pray there sincerely, ever having in his heart the praise of the Lord. This insistence on the external ritual of church attendance and true confession is a vital one in the whole moralising philosophy of Repentance of which the Orders were such great champions:

---

[1] See the edition by Meyer and Toulmin Smith, pp. 44–45.
[2] See the edition by Welter, pp. 55–56 ('De executoribus malis et eorum periculis').

Bone vie est de amer
Deu e homme de bon quer,
Volenters aler a mousters

44

E la dyre ses prieres,
Haÿr pecché e vylenye,
Loaunge de [Deu en] ceste vie

(fol. 84ʳ)

En quer aver e afforcer,

48

A charité [suvent duner]³
De bens leaument purchacez,
Hou poveres partyr en privetez,
Mal recevere sanz mal fere.

52

Une teus homme put Deu plere.

— thus the good man must also be humble and heedless of material wealth: he may accumulate legitimate goods, but must give generously to charity; he must be prepared to share with the poor in privacy and brotherhood, and be ready to turn the other cheek when wronged. Such is the character of a man pleasing in the sight both of the Lord and of Nicholas Bozon.

An appropriately calm and solemn note has entered the sermon; but Bozon would not be a good preacher if he were to lay down his cutting edge too soon. Faithful to his sense of parallelism and apt antithesis, he instantly counters this fine and approving picture with a sharp portrayal of the 'bad life'; and yet again one may imagine him looking pointedly around his shuffling congregation. This renewed assault follows on quite logically from the poem's original title-theme, Bozon stating that overt acts of religion, like large legacies, are purely and inadequately cosmetic if they are not supported by true feeling and behaviour:

Hore quident plusours de male vie
Sentefyer lur ribaudie
Par cynkaunteyne de 'Ave Maries',

56

Hou par aumoyne un poy de myes,
Hou par june de Nostre Dame.

— these people reckon to license their immorality with a string of Hail Maries, a crumb-scattering of alms or a little fasting. This is cynical incon-

---

³ The reading of the MS at this point is clearly unsatisfactory: *loaunge de ceste vie* / (fol. 84ʳ) *en quer aver e afforcer a charité* represent vv. 46–48 in the text, and are written with extra spacing that hints at a scribal lacuna possibly occasioned by the switch from the foot of one folio to the top of the next. The suggested reconstruction of the lines in question is based partly on the logical sense of the passage, and on the example of v. 65, *a freres doune de ses bens.* . . .

sistency verging upon the hypocritical, and all the more to be condemned.
It was of course the great message of the Orders in the thirteenth century
that acts of penance are meaningful only if they follow true and sincere
confession; as the admonishing hermit points out to the sinful baron in the
great OF moralising poem *Le Chevalier au Barisel*:

> 'Or voi je bien que Diex te het.
> Te penitance riens ne set,
> Car tu l'as fait sans repentance
> Et sains amour et sains pitance . . .'.[4]

So Bozon sketches a merciless portrait of the sinner who is quite heedless of his bad reputation; who offers a few pence to St Andrew, but
swears and blasphemes all day long; who lights a candle in church, but still
openly curses his neighbour; who funds a hospice for the poor, but does
not think to curb his lewd language; who gives largesse to the friars, but
treats his serfs like dogs (a personal observation from the radical Franciscan); who persists in his *lecherie*, his wanton self-indulgence, despite
making over-ready gifts of cash:

> Force ne funt de mal fame.
> Pur un dener a seynt Andreu
> 60   Cent feez le jour parjuren[t] Deu;
> Trouve hun cerge devaunt la croyz,
> E maudit sun preme de haute voiz;
> Quater poveres en sale peit,
> 64   E de orde parole ne tent ja plet;
> A freres doune de ses bens
> E tent s[es] paysanz vil cum chens;
> Pur un dener a [c]haut pas
> 68   Sa lecherie ne lerra pas.

– Bozon's sermon against over-reliance on financial pseudo-penances
has ended by focussing upon *ribaudie* and *lecherie*: in common with all his
fellow-moralists he holds depravity in particular contempt (the *Tabula
exemplorum* dismisses debauched sinners as the devil's swine, wallowing in
filth),[5] and devotes two of his *Contes* to the subject, both illustrated with
memorable Bestiary-images. In the one, he likens 'luxuriosos' to rutting
stags, pawing the ground and losing the appetite to eat: 'Auxint le lechour
perde talent de espiritel manger';[6] while in the other he describes that

---

[4] See the edition by Lecoy, vv. 779–82.
[5] See the edition by Welter, p. 43.
[6] See the edition by Meyer and Toulmin Smith, p. 56 ('Contra luxuriosos').

symbol of lust, the hedgehog, and its habit of carrying a mass of apples on its spines: 'Auxint est del lecheour, auxint est del trechour: ove tote la charge q'eux portent de peché, uncore ne sount il paiez. . . .'[7]

The sermon concludes with an uncompromising warning to the heedless sinner, but on a significantly modest note by Friar Nicholas, who begs his audience to pray for him:

> Tele chose ne vaut ren,
> Sanz lesser le mal e fere le ben.
> Pryez Deu pur Bosoune
> 72 Ke vous fet ceo sarmoun.
>   AMEN.

This seventh poem, with its initial image of the useless Last Will and Testament, has had the figure of Death ever in the background. The next poem concentrates upon it: its theme is Mutability.

---

[7] See the edition by Meyer and Toulmin Smith, p. 88 ('Contra luxuriosos et maliciosos').

THE EIGHTH SERMON:
PREPARE FOR DEATH

*(Vous purveez en ceste vie
de soustenaunce en l'autre vie.)*

Nicholas Bozon's 'signature' at the end of the previous text led early students of the manuscript to assume that this was the final sermon of the sequence; in so doing, they failed to take account of the two further poems following directly on from fol. 84^r, similarly introduced by a moral rubric, and each bearing the clear hallmark of Bozon's authorship in both matter and style. The sequence is thus certainly of nine texts and not of seven, and this is accepted by modern authorities; the presence of the friar's name in the seventh sermon no more implies an overall conclusion than does its previous insertion at the end of the second.

This eighth sermon does, however, differ from all its companions in one important respect: it is preserved in two other manuscripts apart from MS British Library Additional 46919 that alone contains the complete sermon-sequence: MS Lambeth Palace Library 522 fols 220^v-222^r, and MS British Library Sloane 1611 fol. 68^v. As the poem is extremely accomplished, and deals with the great medieval moralising theme of man's preparation in earthly life for the life to come, its presence in more than one manuscript is not in itself a matter for great surprise. There is, however, a complication: whereas the Lambeth and Sloane versions clearly support each other in every respect, the poem offered by MS Additional 46919 shows a number of unique and serious variants, that make its choice as base text a dubious one. The Lambeth version has been chosen to illustrate this chapter, on three main counts: firstly, it is the oldest, dating from the later thirteenth century (and pushing the chronology of Bozon's earlier work positively before 1300); secondly, the language is clearer and the presentation more logically ordered than in Additional 46919; thirdly, all its readings are confirmed by Sloane 1611.

MS Lambeth Palace Library 522 is, like Additional 46919, a small but thick volume (320 folios, 22 cm × 13 cm), containing much material of Franciscan provenance and inspiration. It is the product of a single Anglo-Norman scribe of the thirteenth century, writing in a large hand that allows eighteen lines to the page; there are a number of initial illuminations, of good quality. The manuscript's main text is Robert Grosseteste's allegorical *Chasteau d'Amour*; it also contains a 600-line poem by Thibaut de Marly on the state of the world, and an Anglo-Norman version of the *Evangile de Nicodème*. The rest of the manuscript is effectively given over to a large number of Anglo-Norman devotional verses: poems to Christ and to the Virgin, saints' litanies, confessional texts (some pieces are written out twice).[1] Bozon's sermon (lacking the introductory rubric peculiar to the nine texts of Additional 46919) is written as prose, with the stanzas indicated by paragraph-marks; the refrain is omitted by the copyist until after the fifth stanza: then and subsequently it is indicated by its opening word, and is not written out in full until the end. The text is preceded by a common verse prayer of supplication to the Virgin (fol. 220^r) and followed, on fol. 222^r, by a devotional poem on the Passion. As it stands in this earliest form, it consists of ten lyric stanzas of double tailed-couplets, with the tail-rhyme remaining constant throughout; there is a refrain of three lines: a tailed couplet taking up the rhyme of the tail-lines in the stanzas. Bozon's use of a refrain here is particularly skilled: it is bound into the stanzas not merely by the rhyme-repeat, but by the frequent echo in the rest of the poem of its opening word *Chescun*. . . .

The poem falls into four carefully-presented and logically successive parts that reflect Bozon's rhetorical skill as a preacher, as well as his mastery of the lyric form. The first three stanzas introduce the theme with the image of husbandry already observed in the fifth sermon; the uncompromising opening statement of man's inevitable death leads on to the clear warning that he should look to his fate in the hereafter, and take care to store up and save his good deeds against future needs:

I   Puis ke homme deit de ci partyr
        E en ceste vie murir,
           E aillurs sanz fin remeyndra,
4   Bon serreit ke chescun trussast
        Les biens ke il peust mettre en sun sac,
           Kar jamés ci ne revendra.
                Chescun pense del espleiter
                ke il ne perde le grant luer
                    ke Jesu Crist promis nos ad.

— it may be seen that the refrain constantly urges the listener to think to his achievements if he wishes to be saved; here as elsewhere, Bozon employs the motif of *luer/louhier*, the reward bestowed by Heaven upon those

---

[1] For details of the contents, see R. Reinsch, 'Mittheilungen aus einer franz. Handschrift des Lambeth Palace zu London', *ASNS*, 63 (1880), 51–96; and M. R. James, *Descriptive Catalogue of Manuscripts in Lambeth Palace Library* (Cambridge, 1932), pp. 715–23.

who show sufficient merit. The image of the sack of good acts is strength-
ened in an agricultural context in the second stanza where the poet takes
up his favoured theme of harvest and sustenance, with the month of
August in evidence, as it is in the fifth sermon:

II	Aust signifie ceste vie:
8	Li sage en aust fait la quillie
	Dunt il en le an vivera;
	E la petite formie
	En esté pas ne se oblie:
12	Bien seit ke yvern aprés vendra. (Refrain)

Here the allegory of the *quillie*, the gathering-in of the harvest, has been
reinforced by the Biblical image of the wise ant, a character that appears
in a comparable homiletic context in the *Contes moralisés*:

La fourmye est de tiel nature qe greyn ne quiert fors greyn de fur-
ment, e soun purchace met en privé lieu par dedens soun clos pur
sauver le de vent, qe ne soit emportee.... Tiel deit estre la vie de prod-
homme: rien desirer fors qe bountee....[2]

The allegory of husbandry is continued into the third stanza, with heart-
searching men, young and old, likened to gleaners laying up store for the
future:

III	Chescun veye en sen corage,
	Li jevenes e li veus de age,
	En queu biens se afiera;
16	Chescun veie ke il ad glené,
	E quels biens il a ci entassé,
	E queus biens od lui menera. (Refrain)

— by dint of careful repetition, the poem is developing around the concept of *biens*, shifting from the representation of spiritual assets (the metaphor being greatly helped by the play on 'goods'/'goodnesses'), to the
literal sense of 'material possessions'. The next three stanzas sound the
warning of the uselessness of worldly goods, and present a typical Franciscan moral against egoism and vanity; woes accumulate from birth to death,
and even he who recognises his state and fate is scarcely vouchsafed any joy:

IV	Chescun pense ke od doil nasqui,
20	Od doil e od tristur vit issi,
	Od (fol. 221^1) doil s'en departyra;

[2] See the edition by Meyer and Toulmin Smith, p. 89 ('Quod bonum cupiatur et
vana gloria fugiatur').

> Vie de homme n'est for dolur,
> A peyne joie avera un sul jur
> 24   Ke de sa fyn bien pensera. (Refrain)

— the picture is deliberately bleak, with its repeated vocabulary of sadness and pain; and this note is rendered even harsher in the next stanza by a very medieval stress on physical decay, against which neither might nor valour, gold nor silver, is proof:

> V   Quei vaut force u pruesce?
>   Ke vaut aver u richesce?
>   Or e argent, tuit se irra.
> 28   E li cors irra purrir en terre,
>   E le alme irra grant erre,
>   Trussé de ceo ke ele glena. (Refrain)

— the contrast is made between the destruction of the defenceless body rotting in the earth and the state of the soul at least supported by whatever has been stored up in its favour. Bozon has retained the imagery of husbandry to depict the soul as a gleaner trudging a long homeward journey bearing his full sack on his back; and the message of the opening stanza returns with its initial motif and with renewed vigour, as death puts in a more direct appearance, however long-lived, rich or powerful a man may be:

> VI   Puis ke home avra vesqui cent anz,
> 32   Ja n'ert tant prus ne tant vaillanz,
>   Ne tant de richesces en avera,
>   Ke tuit nel perde a un launz,
>   Kar mort tapit en mi sun gaunt,
> 36   Kant meyns quide [le prendera].[3] (Refrain)

In his first sermon, Bozon has likened death to a *laroun* (v. 111), and here he employs the same personification: death is a grim footpad, lurking to pounce unexpectedly, sooner or later, upon the very highest and wealthiest, who will suddenly be stripped of everything.

This reference to the briefly-held vanity of the rich and the noble leads on to the next stage of Bozon's lyric sermon, to stanzas VII and VIII which together form an ominous reminder of the Day of Judgement, before which all the mightiest 'Etats du monde' will be powerless: kings and lords, clerics and scholars. Bozon again joins the ranks of the Franciscan

---

[3] MS Lambeth Palace 522 omits *le prendera*; reading from MSS Sloane 1611 and Additional 46919.

moralisers in seeking to pull down the most powerful and worldly from
the sheer egoism of their high posts:

	VII	Ke fra li roys, barun u cuntes,
		Ke riens ne sievent des acuntes?
		Acunter lur covendra.
40		Certes, mult averunt grant hunte,
(fol. 221ᵛ)		Ne lur vendra cuntur ne cunte:
		Chescun por sei respondera. (Refrain)
	VIII	Ke fra li eveske e li erceveske,
44		Ke li bons clers, u li sage mestre
		Ke tant des acuntes apris ad?
		Kant la summe iert de lui sustrete,
		De despenses e de receite,
48		Li plus sage a fols se tendra. (Refrain)

With his talent for the striking metaphor Bozon here employs the dual
image (punning in the original) of the lawcourt and the counting-house:
these rich sinners' debits outstrip their credits, their books are not in
order, and no lawyer will speak for them at the bankruptcy hearing. Such
people are indeed aptly 'brought to account', and Bozon has sardonic fun
in showing how the illiterate lord baron is at one in confusion with the
lord bishop or with the learned scholar, the *sage mestre* whose head may
have been stuffed with facts and figures (*acuntes*), but who still has to
admit his folly as he ends up a spiritual debtor. The preaching friars'
attacks on worldly pomp do not spare intellectual arrogance: one *exemplum* tells of a bishop who praises two scholars of Divinity for their vir-
tuous works, but reproves a third; when the latter protests hotly that he is
far more learned than the others, the bishop answers that the Devil himself is reckoned a great theologian, while a coarse sack may contain the
best grain.[4]

Bozon's detailed metaphor of accountancy in these stanzas is of some
extra interest when one realises that the Franciscans had from 1260 laid
down firm rules for proper book-keeping within the Order; each house was
supposed to look to its own accounts, note income and expenditure and
present the figures for audit.[5] Having found themselves willy-nilly, for all
their praise of poverty, involved in financial transactions, the friars seem to
have made an official effort to keep such inevitable dealings under control.
The poet's choice of imagery and his handling of technical vocabulary may
partly reflect this effort.

---

[4] *Tabula exemplorum*, edited by Welter, p. 75 ('Scientia').
[5] Cf. Moorman, *A History of the Franciscan Order ...* , pp. 355–57.

As for the legal figure of Counsel, representing the other half of Bozon's punning imagery, the *cuntur* reappears in the *Contes moralisés* once as a wise man profiting from example, but more often as the subtle Silvertongue destined for hell.[6] The Devil-huntsman's fourth pet dog is unleashed against the lawyers who are condemned by their inflated sense of self-importance:

> . . . Un autre chien ad puis descouplé, qe Baudewyn est apellé, a pledours e a legistres e a countours, dount plusours sount chacez en enfer par baudour de lur sen.[7]

— in this Bozon is one of many medieval preachers and moralisers who do not stint themselves in their often savage criticism of the legal profession; the lawyers are prime targets on various counts, not the least being their extracting of fat purses from their clients and their willingness to twist justice to serve their own ends. Jacques de Vitry tells how an advocate whose tongue was always busy slandering others loses it in death;[8] and elsewhere describes Nero in Hell, bathing in molten gold and inviting a group of lawyers to join him — he has reserved a place for such men.[9] The *Liber exemplorum* retells this story, and adds a good half dozen other exempla besides, citing contemporary names and places for authenticity's sake.[1] The *Tabula exemplorum* accuses lawyers of acting for both sides and of failing to maintain decent standards of justice;[11] and John de Bromyard predictably directs a stream of invective against the profession in his *Summa Predicantium.*[12] To these collections may be added the assaults of Etienne de Fougieres, Guiot de Provins, Rutebeuf — an almost endless satirical list.

Bozon's poem ends on the required note of exhortation to shun worldly sin, to direct one's life towards good and to place one's faith in Christ, for the soul can rely at death on no other support. The chosen allegory is that of the chivalrous quest; steadfast knighthood and true service to the Lord are rewarded, but hell awaits him whose life is consumed by vice:

> IX   Vie de homme, c'est chevalerie:
>   Ki bien la gard, e dreit la guie,
>   Grant luer de Deu avera.

---

[6] Contrast the 'sages countours e pledours e bailifs' of No. 126 with '. . . les uns advocatz, countours, legistrers e pledours e les gence qe sount en dozeyns' who are attacked in No. 2 (*Contra advocatos, legistas et juratos*); edited by Meyer and Toulmin Smith, pp. 149, 9.

[7] Ibid., p. 32.

[8] *Sermones communes,* edited by Greven, p. 12.

[9] *Sermones vulgares,* edited by Crane, p. 14.

[10] See the edition by Little, pp. 40–43.

[11] See the edition by Welter, p. 2.

[12] See Owst, *Literature & Pulpit . . .* , pp. 345–48.

52   E ki degaste sa vie
En peché e en vilaynie,
      En enfern ostel prendra. (Refrain)

X   Seyngnur, ky voit en ceste vie
56   Servir Jhesu le fiz Marie,
      Sachez ke grant luer avera;
Car kant le alme iert du cors partye,
Dunc n'avera ele ami ne amie,
60   Alas! en ki se afiera.
(fol. 222ʳ)   Chescun pense del espleiter
      ke il ne perde le grant luer
      ke Jesu Crist promis nos ad.

In addressing his audience in these final verses, Bozon returns very effectively to the opening image of the *vie de homme*, and also, by means of the repetition of *grant luer* in the feudal context of a true knight's 'guerredon', re-echoes and redoubles at the poem's climax the moral message of the refrain, with its promise of God's reward.

The version of this sermon-lyric supplied by MS British Library Sloane 1611 follows the Lambeth Palace 522 text faithfully, with only the occasional variant prefix (v. 3 *meindra*, v. 15 *se fiera*) or number (vv. 37-38 *cunte* : *acunte*). The text is found on fol. 68ᵛ, the final leaf of a thirteenth-century French book of Latin liturgical hymns originally independent of the rest of the manuscript with which it is now bound, and which contains two OF treatises on medicine and an OF verse *Life* of St. Margaret.[13] The poem has been written by a later, fourteenth-century English hand in the space available on this final folio, not without difficulty: beginning on the near-blank column *d*, and setting the poem as prose (with each stanza forming a paragraph), the copyist has reached the foot of the folio with two stanzas remaining, which he is forced to cram in the marginal space beneath the existing column *c*. Finally the whole refrain, hitherto omitted, has been written in one line along the foot of the leaf, perilously near the edge. The text's exposed position has left it in a bad state: parts of the final stanzas and the refrain, though recognisable in context, have worn away to near-illegibility.

When one comes to consider the Additional 46919 version, headed by the customary rubric-couplet already cited, one glance at the text beyond the opening stanza is sufficient to recognise the extent to which it differs from Lambeth/Sloane; in the first place the careful composition of the

[13] See P. Meyer, 'Notice du MS. Sloane 1611 du Musée Britannique', *Romania*, 40 (1911), 532-35.

stanzas has been dispersed like so many shuffled cards, and in the second two extra stanzas have been added to the pack. The following concordance sets out the variations (the Lambeth and Sloane manuscripts are given the *sigles A* and *B*, and the Additional 46919 version is denoted by *C*):

AB		C
I		I
II		XI
III		XII
IV		II
V		III
VI	(in part)	VIII
VII		VI
VIII		VII
IX	(in part)	V
X	(in part)	IX
–		(IV)
–		(X)

Instead of the logical four-part construction of *AB*, *C* offers a rhetoric that is constantly chopping and changing. The opening image of husbandry is limited to the first stanza, which is immediately followed by the theme of the pain of life and the vanity of wealth. A new stanza (IV) recapitulates the imagery of man taking his good deeds with him beyond death. These are the only 'possessions' the wise traveller should rely on, and these he will find ready to hand:

> S'avise chescun, et fra ke sage,
> Avaunt ke veygne au passage
> En queu bens s'afiera:
> Les benfez ke avera fet icy
> Prest les trovera devaunt ly
> Kaunt du secle departyra . . .

– and the poem then moves straight to the exhortatory contrast between heaven's rewards to the good and hellfire for the sinners. There next follow the two stanzas on the ill-prepared Estates, before the poet switches back to the inevitability of lurking death, and then returns once more to the concept of the value of good deeds to the isolated and exposed soul. An extra stanza (X) provides a new exhortation to all to reflect well and not to doubt the poet's words, for each shall receive his just deserts:

> Pur ceo checun se purvee,
> E ceo ke ay dit ne descreye,
> Kar tout yssi serra;
> Ceo ke homme avera cy overé
> Ayllours ly ert gueridouné:
> Teu fet, teu louher recevera . . .

– and the poem ends with a sudden return to the opening theme of the gleaning soul, with the images of harvest, the ant and the sack of good deeds.

C undoubtedly has power and vigour, but lacks the smooth coherence of *AB*; in particular it has lost the very important climax of the poet's dramatic address to his listeners in which he urges them to serve *Jhesu le fiz Marie*. The two extra stanzas do not add anything new to the poem (and stanza IV rather lamely repeats elements found elsewhere, in stanzas I and XII); and in stanza II C has reversed the order of the two sets of tailed couplets as found in the corresponding stanza IV of *AB*, destroying their logical progression (from the images of pain to the summing-up: *Vie de homme n'est for dolur* . . . , and so to the proposed sensible course).

There are many other variants; as the concordance shows, three further stanzas correspond in the two versions only partly. Stanza VI of *AB* is found in the following form as stanza VIII of C:

> Seyt homme veuz hou enfaunt,
> Ja si fort ne wayllanz,
>   Ke il ne mourra;
> La mort tapit dedenz sé gaunz,
> Ke ly ferra de sa launz,
>   Kaunt meynz quyde le prendera . . .

— there is no man, young or old, however strong or valiant he may be, who will not die; at this point the original stressed ironic transition from wealth and wellbeing to sudden disaster (*ke tuit nel perde a un launz* . . .) has been lost, and the figure of death brought more melodramatically into the foreground by the reworking of *launz* ('swoop') to mean 'lance' and the subsequent altering of the whole image to fit a new tournament-context. Again, stanza IX of *AB* is represented in C by the far less allegorical stanza V, containing a straight contrast between the heavenly reward of the good man and the eternal hell awaiting the sinner:

> Ke si cum cely ke ben fet
> Le ceel pur louher, cum promis est,
>   Recevera,
> Ausi cely ke sa vie
> Desgaste en pecché e vylenye
>   En enfern demorra . . .

— and stanza X of *AB* loses its preaching address in the course of its transition to the somewhat repetitive stanza IX of C, stating that one good deed in life is better and of greater comfort than ten afterwards:

> Meuz vaut un ben devaunt la mort
> Ke dis aprés, et plus cumfort
>   L'alme kant s'en irra.
> Kant l'alme ert departye,
> Ne avera dounke amye (*sic*) ne amye,
>   Allas! en ky s'afiera . . .

If the case for *A* as base text is reasonably made, the fact remains that *C* presents a perversely intriguing variant, particularly given its privileged situation surrounded by the other poems of Bozon's sermon-sequence. Does it, with its deliberately shuffled stanzas and extra images, represent the poet's own later emended version of a text originally composed as an independent lyric? It is after all the one sermon in the sequence with a lyric refrain. If Bozon has in fact had second thoughts and reworked an earlier piece, adding dramatic emphasis and repetition, and restructuring the text cyclically rather than progressively, it may critically be argued that he has not improved upon his first draft.

When all is said, however, it should be noted that this particular *C* version of Bozon's poem did not lack contemporary acclaim: it was actually translated into English by his fellow-Franciscan, William Herebert, the early fourteenth-century owner of MS British Library Additional 46919. The translation is found at fols 208ᵛ-209ʳ of the manuscript among Herebert's own autograph collection of his English compositions, and is a faithful rendering of form and content. It is introduced, like the Anglo-Norman original, by a rubric:

> *Bysoeth ʒon in þysylke lyf*
> *of lyflode in þat oþer lyf.*

— and an opening excerpt is sufficient to reveal the neatness of the translation:

> Soethye mon shal hoenne wende
> And nede deʒen at þen ende
> And wonyen he not whare,
> God ys þat he trusse hys pak
> And tymliche put hys stor in sak
> Þat not when hoenne vare.
> Oeuch mon þenche uor to spede
> þat he ne loese þe grete mede
> þat God ous dythte ʒare. . . .[14]

It is a fair compliment to Nicholas Bozon; and Herebert's interest will again be in evidence, marginally at least, in the final sermon.

[14] See C. Brown and R. H. Robbins, *The Index of Middle English Verse* (New York, 1943), no. 3135; and R. H. Robbins, 'Friar Herebert and the Carol', *Anglia*, 75 (1957), 194–98.

THE NINTH SERMON:
THE HUMBLE AND THE HYPOCRITICAL

Ke plusours unt aÿe
par un homme de bone vie.

With his final verse sermon Nicholas Bozon returns, at least initially,
to his ideal of the 'honnête homme' *de bone vie*, whose shining example he
has praised throughout his texts, in sore contrast to the sinning behaviour
of his congregation. In order to make this contrast all the sharper, he inter-
leaves a sober expression of the Franciscan message that the most lowly
and humble may be the closest to God with a full-blooded allegory against
the vice of hypocrisy; and here he reveals all his considerable talent for the
suddenly striking, for the unusual approach, for vivid details enlivening the
sermon in order to capture attention at a crucial moment.

The opening lines sketch out once more the figure of the Good Man,
with the added element of the Franciscan sense of brotherhood; one worthy
individual may bring succour to many of his fellows, indeed to an entire
country. Bozon elaborates on this thesis, using the social example as a
stepping-stone to the religious level:

	Un prodom en compaignie
	A plusours autres fet aÿe:
	Par une homme de bounté
4	Put un paÿs estre sauvé;
	En escripture est trové,
	E par assay est prové.
	Par taunt say la verité:
8	Si hore ne fut une poynnee
	De bone genz entremedlé
	A grant noumbre trop soylee,
	Deu preÿt vengaunce ben sovent
12	De ceo munde par gref tourment.

— were it not for the fact that among the great mass of sinning human-
ity there is a scattering of such redeeming people, the world would have
been doomed to the bitter torment of God's vengeance. Bozon's train of
thought, inspired perhaps by the cautionary example of the destruction of
the Cities of the Plain for the want of just such a *poynnee*, or by the *escrip-*
ture of John 11. 50-51 that shows the one *homme de bounté* to be Jesus

('. . . that one man die that the whole nation perish not . . .'), leads him into a further chain of analogies, increasingly political: a man may be saved from being trampled underfoot by the timely action of his neighbour. Indeed, salvation may come from the least likely quarter, and a tyrant's evil may be palliated by the charity of a single peasant; and this argument is at once elevated to a semi-mystical plane with the introduction of one of the key motifs of repentance, the humility of the saving tear quenching all the flames of sinful acts:

<blockquote>
Kar ben savez ke averouns trové
[Ke] par sun vesyn le bon[té]
Garauntizoun [un homme prent] [1]
16   Ke n'est defolee de la gent.
Dount la bounté de un paysaunt
La malice sauve du tyrant;
Penaunce e lermes du ploraunt
20   Esteynt la flamme de mefesaunz.
</blockquote>

Bozon continues in similar vein, all the time stressing the spiritual ascendancy of humility. None (save all-seeing God alone) may tell who it is that has gained the most merited place (*tenir lieu*) through his qualities and conduct in life; thus it is that he who has remained of little account but who has undergone grievous suffering, may yet be worthier than a hundred others of far greater social standing in this world:

<blockquote>
Pur ceo n'est homme ke pusse ver[2]
— For soul Deu, ke tut put ver —
Ky est cely ke plus teent lu
24   Par sa vie e par sa vertu.
Teus est celee de ky n'est counte,
Mes par aventure sufre hounte,
Ke plus teent a tote la tere
28   Ke cent a[t]res de grant afere.
</blockquote>

— as a true Franciscan, Bozon is intent on cutting the high and mighty down to size (not for nothing are some of his *Contes moralisés* entitled

---

[1] After v. 13 and before v. 16 the MS has the reading: *garauntizoun par sun vesyn le bon*, which is clearly insufficient. The suggested reconstruction of the two necessary lines that have been partly lost is a tentative one, that seeks to preserve both rhyme and meaning. The choice of *prent* is suggested by the comparable OF expressions *prendre damaige/gloire/amendise/penitence* (compare Tobler-Lommatzsch VII, 1739: 43; 1740: 15–16, 37; 1748: 32).

[2] The original may have been *pust saver*; the existing bad rhyme *ver : ver* may thus be the fault of the copyist, and not of the poet.

'Contra dominos impios et injustos', 'De malis dominis et iniquis', 'Contra divites pauperes spoliantes' or 'Quod multi nobiles degenerant'). Christ's grace, he declares, is often given to the most despised: that is why one should show kindness to one's neighbour; and he warns his congregation that there are many people considered fine and granted all worldly honour who would be treated quite differently were the truth about them known:

> Lors (fol. 85^r) est bon ke chescun sage
> Ver soun preme eyt bon corage,
> Kar cely ke porte plus despit
> 32   Est sovent meuz de Jhesu Crist;
> E sovent aveent ke tenoums
> A bone genz ke veoums
> Du mounde estre honuree,
> 36   Mes si nous susum la verité
> Nous troveroyum tout autrement
> En la vie de acun gent.

It is at this stage that the preacher is carried away from his earnest opening thesis into a grotesque world of allegory and satire. The point of connection seems evidently to have been his last image of the so-called *bone genz* pretending to be what they are in fact not, and duping society; from here there is but one logical, but very sudden, step to a most withering assault on Hypocrisy and Covetousness.

No other single human vice is more scathingly dealt with by the medieval moralists than that of hypocrisy, bedfellow of pride and egoism. The *Bible* of Guiot de Provins has hypocrisy act the role of one of three ugly sisters:

> Molt sont et laides et cruals
> Ses trois vielles, et desloaus.
> Des trois vielles sai bien les nons:
> La premiere ait non Traïsons,
> Et la secunde Ypocresie,
> La tierce apelle on Symonie ... [3]

— while in a more political context the poet Rutebeuf memorably brands the mendicant opponents of Guillaume de St-Amour and the University masters:

> ... A vous toz faz je ma clamor
> D'Ypocrisie,
> Cousine germaine Heresie,

[3] See the edition by Orr, vv. 1145–50.

> Qui bien a la terre saisie.
>   Tant est grant dame
> Qu'ele en enfer metra mainte ame;
> Maint homme a mis et mainte fame
>   En sa prison. . . .[4]

Among the Franciscan exempla-collections the *Tabula exemplorum* offers a good representation of the range of the preachers' invective. Hypocrisy is successively likened to a counterfeit coin, to an owl dwelling in a church merely in order to drink the oil, to a crab looking in one direction but going in another, to Reynard playing dead, and to an artist who paints flawless portraits but engenders evil sons (and who, when questioned on the paradox, replies: 'It is because I make pictures by day, and children by night').[5]

It is thus only to be expected that Nicholas Bozon should be actively hostile to the vice; in his *Char d'Orgueil*, hypocrisy forms a fitting canopy over Dame Pride's coach:

> . . . Ceo est la ypocrisie ke cele par coverture
> Tuz les pecchez par desuz, chescun sanz blemure . . .[6]

– and in the *Contes moralisés* he delves into the Bestiary tradition, surfacing with an excellent little exemplum of hypocrisy as glow-worm:

> . . . Un' autre nature est de ceo verm qe est appellé en latyn 'eruke' et en engleiz 'glouworm', qar il lust trop cler de nuyt, e quant vient en lumere de jour, si est trové orde best. Tieux sount les ypocritez qe lusent cler par contenaunce: trovez serrount tut autres al jour de veres conisaunce. . . .[7]

In this final sermon, however, his invention excels itself, as he conjures up four monstrous allegorical creatures that cause great confusion, and in whom may be recognised many people:

> 40   Quatre choses funt ennu,
>   Dount plusours pount estre conu:
>   Roungemesere e Kokenplu,
>   Siflevent e Cheftondu.

[4] *Du Pharisien*, edited by Faral and Bastin, vv. 6–13.
[5] See the edition by Welter, p. 40.
[6] See the edition by Vising, vv. 103–04.
[7] 'Contra ypocrisim pretendentes', edited by Meyer and Toulmin Smith, pp. 95–96.

– that is, 'Chewprayer',[8] 'Bedraggled-cock' (one is tempted to translate by the strictly inexact but certainly appropriate modern term: 'Poppycock'), 'Whistlewind' and 'Shavenpate'. These wonderful characters have immediately appealed to Friar William Herebert, who numbers them one to four in the margin of the manuscript and jots down a fair translation of vv. 39–42 at the foot of fol. 85ʳ:

> Vour thynges ȝe ofte ysoeth,
> Wharethorou monye onknowe boeth:
> Vreteboede, Byrinekoc,
> Whystlebone and Shorelok.

All four names are synonymous not merely with hypocrisy in general, but with religious hypocrisy, or Tartufferie, in particular; their contemporary currency is attested by a strikingly similar list contained in a piece against hypocrisy found on fol. 182ᵛ of MS British Library Harley 505, among some Latin sermons composed in England and dating from the end of the thirteenth century and the beginning of the fourteenth:

> ... contra quod peccat ypocrisis cum septem speciebus que sic gallice dicuntur: singuler, suilevent, cokenplu, geroune, ordbost, roungemysire, coupetout. Isti sunt qui querunt vocari ab hominibus 'Rabi', longas protractando orationes ...[9]

– this means that Bozon the friar is pointing his accusing finger very much at his fellow-priests, or rather at those who are not worthy of their cloth. The picture he goes on to paint has more than one detail in common with the stock fabliau character of the *moine* or *provere*; in line before our eyes file four thoroughly unpleasant and unctuous clerics.

Roungemesere/'Vreteboede' is quite literally one who 'makes a meal' of his devotions, who offers an excessive show of piety; Bozon depicts him accordingly kneeling for long hours in prayer, and prostrating himself before the altar:

> Roungemesere fet semblaunt
> 44   De longe priere en genulant:

---

[8] That this is the sense of the nickname (*mesere* standing for *meserere*) is shown by the context and by Herebert's literal ME translation (see below); one may, however, note a punning connection with 'misère'.

[9] P. Meyer, 'Extraits d'un recueil de sermons latins composés en Angleterre', *Romania*, 35 (1906), 590–96. Among the other names in this list may be recognised 'Blame-all' (*Coupetout*), 'Trimmer' (*Suilevent*), and possibly 'Selfseeker' (*Singuler*) and 'Filthypride' (*Ordbost* [?]). *Geroune* is the plant *arum maculatum*, or Cuckoo-pint; for the significance of weeds denoting envy or hypocrisy, see below.

Devant le auter en croupisouns
Git cum fut en oreysouns.

— yet it is all in pretence, all contrived in order to dupe folk into think-
ing him a truly devout priest. Any living, any benefice left unclaimed by
'Chewprayer' is instantly seized by *Sir Kokenplu*/'Byrinekoc', whose capi-
tal attribute is to present a most poor, wretched and unworldly mien while
all the time hugging to his breast envy, pride and ambition; he may seem
to care not a shred for his appearance, but his humility is a feigned one in
order to gain an undeserved reputation for holiness, like some tattered hermit from the pages of the *Vitae Patrum*:

	Sy nule rente seyt vacaunt
48	Ke Roungemesere seit mis avaunt,
	Dunt s'en veent sire Kokenplu,
	Ke force ne fet cum seit vestu;
	Partut oblye honesteté
52	Pur aver los de seynteté.

'Coc empleu', the bird soaking, drenched: the OF equivalent of the
modern 'poule mouillée'; while the later expression describes someone
timorous or cowardly, the medieval *coc empleu* has moved from the original sense of one downcast or dejected to that of hypocrite, fit synonym
for the ubiquitous *papelard*. Bozon glosses the image expertly: his character's priestly garment hangs dishevelled upon him like a bedraggled cock's
wings; and he takes great and deceitful care to appear unworldly and preoccupied by his devotions, while in fact he is gloating, and preening himself inside, the very embodiment of the maxim 'l'habit ne fait pas le
moine':

	Ses heles pent cum fet le kok
	Kant est enplu de amerok.
	Devant la gent se fet pensifs,
56	Tut eyt il le quer jolifs:
	S'en ad contrefet ke n'ad ke fere
	De ren ke seyt cy en tere.

— Bozon seems here to be punning on the twin parallel meanings of
enplu: drenched from without, and sodden from within (as with wine).
The cock is thus also suffering the effects of an excess of *amerok*; Bozon's
use of the term deserves some consideration, as it adds an important evocative element to the portrait of this Tartuffe of the fourteenth century.
Ameroc (Med. Lat. *Amerusca*) is the plant *Anthemis cotula*, known in

English as 'Mayweed', 'Houndfennel' or 'Stinking Camomile'. It appears to have been commonly used in medieval folk-medicine; in a ME adaptation of Walter de Henley's treatise on husbandry we read:

> ... geder ... in herveste ... ameroch, oþer wise callid maydens wede, & dry it & at þe firste comynge in to þe howse of your shepe ... let þis erbe be medled withe þer haye ... it will dry þe evyll humore þat is withe in þer bodies ...[10]

— and elsewhere it is cited as a proof against constipation: '... ȝif þou be costyf and wolt make nesche þe wombe, take mathnes [ME term for 'mayweed'] and seþ hem ... and et þer-of. ...'[11]

However, *in situ* Ameroc is considered an undesirable weed, a pest to be rooted out; witness Walter de Bibbesworth, in his Anglo-Norman treatise on the French Language (c. 1280–90):

> ... E si vous trovez au verger
> Ameroke e gletoner,
> Les arassez de une besagu,
> E plauntez cholet en leur liu ...[12]

— the *gletoner* with which the ameroc is here associated is the burr (*Lappa*), which notoriously sticks to anyone passing through a field; *ameroke* is evidently in very bad company.

Anthemis cotula is indeed a common weed in arable land; it is also unpleasantly smelly, particularly when bruised (hence 'Stinking camomile'). This distasteful property carries us closer to the plant's symbolic application in Bozon's sermon. The actual point of contact is to be found in another poem by Bozon, the allegorical *Char d'Orgueil*; in the course of his description of Envy, the fourth horse that draws Dame Pride's coach ('Mult est male beste ...'), the friar states:

> ... Nule rien ne vult manger for ke haveroun,
> Ameroke e cherderye, c'est detraccion.
> Pus si est enbeveré de mal suspecioun,
> [E] de un torchet correyé de purpens feloun ...[13]

— so it may be seen that in Bozon's mind here *ameroc* is fit only for

---

[10] See the edition by Lamond, p. 56.

[11] G. Henslow, *Medical Works of the Fourteenth Century* (London, 1899), 12/10.

[12] See the edition by A. Owen (Paris, 1929), vv. 665–68 (section dealing with plant-names).

[13] See the edition by Vising, vv. 237–40. It may be noted that a text of this poem is found in MS British Library Additional 46919, with the relevant stanza appearing at fol. 69ᵛ, just a few folios before our verse sermon; the two uses of *ameroc* are thus in close proximity.

foul creatures, and — as Envy's food — stands symbolically for 'detraction', or disparagement (a vice often condemned by the preachers). It is furthermore associated in this context with two new items, *haveroun* and *cherderye*, that lead still deeper into the world of medieval symbolism. '*Haveroun*' (or *Averun/Abroigne*) is the plant *Artemisia abrotanum*, 'Southernwood'; it has an agreeable camphor-and-lemon odour, and is also found as a healing herb in early medicine, but all this belies its highly unpleasant and bitter taste; it is in fact of the same genus as *Absinthium*, Wormwood — which, with its partner Gall, is commonly and allegorically associated with the vice of envy. Evidently its bitterness makes it a fit fruit for the horse Envy, together with *Ameroc*.

'*Cherderye*' (or *Jargerie/Jazerie/Garberie*) is the common tare. OF texts insist on the need to separate it from wheat ('Ne avoec le forment seme le garberie . . .', etc.); and in this context its unpleasant nature is firmly stressed by its infamous Biblical role (inspired in particular by the parable of Matthew 13. 24–30). With the parable acting as a bridge, the symbolic use of the term enters moralising texts of the thirteenth century:

> . . . Or est bien drois que je vos die que la jargerie et les espines et les maises erbes senefient: la jargerie senefia la male creance . . .[14]

— and in his *Besant Dieu* Guillaume le Clerc retells the parable in an allegory against the daughters of Pride, 'Envie e Luxure e Iveresce':

> . . . Desus le biau furment sema
> Garzerie e droe e neele
> E yveraie, qui la cervele
> E tut le cors de l'home empire . . .[15]

— from here the term passes into a proverbial usage retained in the modern French form 'la zizanie', envious discord.

So '*Ameroc*' is clearly associated with devilish plants of Envy, and its role in Bozon's sermon is quite plain and highly appropriate. Envy and covetousness are part of Kokenplu's hypocrisy: he has already been described as avidly on hand to seize any unclaimed benefice. *Ameroc* is suitable food indeed for his falsely-bedraggled body.

That a Cock should represent a 'faux-dévot' is equally fitting, since in the Middle Ages the bird is frequently found as the symbol of a priest, being the harbinger of light and the awakener from slumber. Nicholas

---

[14] *La vie et la translation de S Jacques le majeur*, edited by P. Meyer, *Romania*, 31 (1902), 252–73 (p. 265).

[15] See the edition by Ruelle, vv. 1592–95; cf. also vv. 1703–06, describing how Satan seeks to thwart divine acts of goodness: 'Mult creist hui ceste garzerie').

Bozon follows here in a sarcastic tradition soon to be shared by Chaucer, who uses the character of Chantecler from the *Roman de Renart* unflatteringly to represent the secular clergy, in his *Nun's Priest's Tale*.[16]

Kokenplu has shuffled away, to be replaced by *Sir Siflevent*,[17] the nickname indicating a cleric who takes care to pray in a loud, sibilant whisper, making sure that all may hear him being pious, like his colleague Roungemesere. Bozon shows him as a consummate actor with his sighs and groans and eyes cast up to the heavens, but as a liar towards God:

	Le terce est sire Siflevent,
60	Ke dit ses prieres overtement:
	Souzpire e geent pitousement,
	E get les euz au firmament.
	En porture se porte seyntement,
64	Mes sa porture vers Deu ment;
	Ben seyt dauber confessioun
	Saunz enporter remissioun,
	Kar yl ad prié Contrition
68	Ke weu ne seyt en sa mesoun.

— his personal act of confession is nothing but a veneer; for him there will be no remission of sin, since he lacks the vital emotion of sincere contrition, as the preacher tartly remarks.

Bozon's listeners would surely catch something still more ominous and evil in Siflevent's hissing tongue; for his mannerism, more than just hypocritical, resembles the sound of a serpent, and thus of the Devil himself. The *Gesta Romanorum* offers a striking example of this association, in its version of the tale of the Harper and the Fishes; as one of the ME translations has it:

> . . . Allas! for while þey smitithe the harpe, *scil.* speke the wordes of god, þere comithe an hisser, *scil.* þe devil, & he whistelithe so swetly þat fisshis, *scil.* synners, herithe no worde of god, but turnithe hem to dilectacion of synne, to whiche the devil temptithe hem. For the devil hissithe be many diverse weyes. . . .[18]

With the arrival of the fourth partner in deceit, *Sir Cheftondu*/'Shorelok',

---

[16] Compare C. R. Dahlberg, 'Chaucer's Cock and Fox', *JEGP*, 53 (1954), 277-90; and M. J. Donovan, 'The Moralité of the Nun's Priest's Sermon', *JEGP*, 52 (1953), 498-508.

[17] William Herebert's translation of the name is particularly felicitous, since he has been able to introduce the actual idea of praying with 'Whystlebone': lit. 'Hiss-prayer'.

[18] *The Early English Versions of the Gesta Romanorum*, edited by S. J. H. Herrtage (London, EETS, 1879), p. 138.

we observe the classic lampooning of the 'faux-dévot' who seeks all the honour due to his tonsured crown, but has none to spare for his Maker. Bozon caustically dismisses him as unfit for his office:

Le quart est sire [Chef] toundu,[19]
Ke ben deit estre entendu
Cely ke coroune ad receu
E poy entent en vertu.
Honour demaunde pur la coroune,
E deshonur a Deu doune,
De ky la vye n'est ordiné
Cum apent a corouné.
Plus vaudreit garder les berbis
Ke de manier le chaliz!
Cum plus est en haut degree,
Plus est mester de garder le pee.

72 (line 72)

76 (line 76)

80 (line 80)

In this fourfold condemnation of false humility precise mention has been made of the hypocritical priest's greed for material gain, as represented by the profitable benefice. Bozon will return to the attack in his *Contes*, citing the iniquity of multiple livings, of rich churches made over to ambitious priests in exchange for money; his Devil-huntsman's third hound is named 'Havegyf' ('Give-and-Take'):

... qel est descouplé sur les abbés, priours e chivalers e damez qe ont eglises en lur donisoun, qe pensent en donant de doner e prendre....[20]

The issue of the plurality of benefices was indeed a thorny one, often enough condemned by the preachers as contrary both to the moral ethic of humble poverty and to Canon Law itself. According to the *Tabula exemplorum*, such grasping priests are like greedy horses, each eating enough for three but failing to do the work of three;[21] and the *Speculum laicorum* tells the story of a high cleric doomed to hell for his vainglory, and for amassing benefices.[22]

The allegory over, Bozon returns to his audience (his attack on religious falseness is plainly addressed as much to the clergy as to the laity, if not more so), and weaves his vivid, farcical example into his homily:

[19] The MS omits 'Chef'.
[20] See the edition by Meyer and Toulmin Smith, p. 31.
[21] See the edition by Welter, p. 73.
[22] See the edition by Welter, pp. 62–63 ('De gaudio vero et falso'). For a survey of other, later English sermons of complaint against clerical greed, see Owst, *Literature and Pulpit* ..., pp. 267–69, 273–75.

> Pur ceo, seygnurs, laÿs e clers,
> Ke avez oÿ ceo quatre vers,
> Countregardés de ypocrisye
> 84   E amez verité de bone vie.
> Avant ke quydent sunt hapez
> Par mort sobit, e enporteez.
> Mort sobite est dreyt nomee
> 88   Kant la vie n'est ordiné
> Avant ke alme yst du corps.

— so the preacher comes back to his recurrent theme of *bone vie*, of the sincerity that alone is proof against hypocrisy, and also once again to that image already tellingly deployed in his sermons of Death as a highwayman lying in wait and pouncing swiftly, and too soon indeed, to seize those hypocrites whose lives have not been properly led, or souls prepared for their departure. With vv. 87-89 Bozon seeks final inspiration from Hélinant's *Vers de la Mort*,[23] developing the borrowed lines further into a dread climax with the inevitable picture of eternal torment:

> Allas! quel houstel trovera lors
> Ycele alme ke issi est passé?
> 92   A mal houre fut crée!
> Homme demurt en soun pecché,
> Kar touz jours saunz fyn est dampné.

Having disposed of his four horsemen of hypocrisy, Bozon concludes on a note of spiritual hope and uplift. He repeats the exhortation of the opening sermon, that one should look to one's earthly deeds and be ready for death with a clear and calm conscience; and his final image is that of God the cleanser, the true *fons et origo*: mankind, soiled by sin's filth, will find purification in the healing waters of the fountain of the Trinity that flows from Father's source to Son's stream and to the mighty river of the Holy Spirit. The soul that refuses this grace must be dark indeed:

> Pur ceo seum touz jours prestez,
> 96   E pernum garde a nos fez
> Ke ne fasum chose pur quay
> La conscyence seyt en affray;
> E si nous seum de ren soyllez
> 100   Par nul ordure de (fol. 85ᵛ) pecché,
> Nous trowum ewe bon e sene
> Ke veent coraunt de la fontaynne.

[23] See the edition by Wulff and Walberg, XXVIII. 1-3.

Li pere est sours, li fiz la veyne,
104   Le seynt esperit la ryvere pleyne
De douce pyté touz jours certeyne.
Mout est alme rude e vyleyne
Ke n'ad ke fere de grace sovereyne.
(108   . . . .)

At this point the sermon ends; the monorhyming of the last seven lines
has provided a deliberate and effective insistence to the conclusion, and (as
in the sixth sermon) concealed the final uneven number. It is possible that
one or more lines may have been lost here (including the terminal 'Amen'),
or as a result of the scribal lacuna of vv. 14–15; but — again as is the case
with the earlier text — there is no obvious break in sense at any point, and
the sermon concludes, quite satisfactorily, on its present note of hope and
warning.

CONCLUSION

So Nicholas Bozon comes to the end of his nine sermons. The subjects have varied from the more venial sins of decorum to the weightier questions of faith, repentance and damnation; but each piece has been stamped with the mark of the professional preacher, the Franciscan well able to put across the vital tenets of his Order in the most direct way possible. He is witty and acerbic, prejudiced but sincere, ever seeking to impress his audience with a particular recognisable image, or to flesh out his sermon with a striking analogy or exemplum. Above all he is observant; through his eyes and his verses we may see real English sinners of the 1300s, uncomfortably present in the preaching-nave of his church as in a Ship of Fools: Jill and Joan chattering together, while their friends preen and flaunt their new dresses; Ralph and John, too smugly conscious of their money-bags to be aware of their envious and hostile kinsfolk; the *juvenceus* itching to be away, their feet tapping a dance-measure; Chewprayer and his fellow-hypocrites, glancing up guiltily from their excessive devotions; the smooth schoolman overconfident in his wisdom, and the coarse countryman neglecting his harvest.

Bozon is at once a down-to-earth onlooker and a medieval intellectual; and it is rewarding to see him continually juxtaposing and blending the two halves of his nature. There is subtlety and Franciscan sophistication behind his trenchant and direct verses; and he is no mean poet. In drawing from the literary fund provided by the *Vers de la Mort*, the *Songe d'Enfer*, or other homiletic texts and exempla-collections, he is never a coarse plagiariser; he incorporates and restructures his material, and transforms it by his personal style. He is a worthy individual entrant to the ranks of those medieval moralists whose impassioned and sometimes shrill voices provide a running commentary on the way of their world. In his works he appears fascinated by his mass of detailed material, and he manages to convey to us through the centuries not a little of this fascination with the bizarre and with the commonplace.

www.ingramcontent.com/pod-product-compliance
Lightning Source LLC
Chambersburg PA
CBHW020238030726
47497CB00009B/3150